D0224389

AdValue

Twenty ways advertising works for business

Edited by
Leslie Butterfield

Published in association with the Institute of Practitioners in Advertising

OXFORD AMSTERDAM BOSTON LONDON NEW YORK PARIS
SAN DIEGO SAN FRANCISCO SINGAPORE SYDNEY TOKYO

Butterworth-Heinemann
An imprint of Elsevier Science
Linacre House, Jordan Hill, Oxford OX2 8DP
200 Wheeler Road, Burlington, MA 01803

First published 2003

British Library Cataloguing in Publication Data
AdValue: Twenty ways advertising works for business
 1. Advertising – Evaluation
 I. Butterfield, Leslie   II. Institute of Practitioners in Advertising
 659.1

Library of Congress Cataloguing in Publication Data
A catalogue record for this book is available from the Library of Congress

ISBN 0 7506 5501 1

For information on all Butterworth-Heinemann publications
visit our website at www.bh.com

Typeset by Keyword Typesetting Services Ltd, Wallington, Surrey
Printed and bound in Great Britain by Biddles Ltd *www.biddles.co.uk*

AdValue

Twenty ways advertising works for business

Contents

Foreword

Hamish Pringle
Director General, IPA

Brands are now generally accepted as among the most valuable assets on many major companies' balance sheets, and the responsibility for managing them often resides at main board level. This means that chief executives and finance directors are called upon to make significant investment decisions on advertising and marketing communications for their brands. Yet, while these decisions are vital to the future prosperity of their businesses and fundamental to protecting and increasing shareholder value, the directors making them are often short of real hands-on marketing experience.

This book, the inspiration of Leslie Butterfield, is designed to provide the reassurance that's required by senior business managers. They know the strength of brands from their own personal experience and the observation of other companies, but need concrete evidence, which is not tied to a particular case history, in order to convince themselves and others of the role for advertising in support of those brands and of their business in general.

Leslie's idea was to produce a series of 'general proofs' of advertising effectiveness. To do so he has marshalled the evidence by asking experts in the field to provide individual chapters (including three of his own), each of which focuses on a particular demonstration of the effectiveness of advertising.

Here 'advertising' is used in its consumer sense, and thus includes all forms of marketing communications. So while each contributor addresses a particular aspect, the whole adds up to a complete overview of how brand communications work and make money for companies.

Our hope is that this new collection of proofs will become a valuable tool for CEOs, FDs, and indeed all directors of companies which own brands and whose future earnings flows will increasingly come from these assets, if they are professionally managed.

Hamish Pringle
Director General, IPA*

*The Institute of Practitioners in Advertising is the industry body and professional institute for UK advertising, media and marketing communications agencies.

Its mission is to serve, promote and anticipate the collective interests of advertising, media and marketing communications agencies, in particular to define, develop and help maintain the highest possible standards of professional practice within the advertising and marketing communications business, negotiating on behalf of its members with media bodies, government departments and unions.

www.ipa.co.uk

Preface
Leslie Butterfield

The big problem with answering the question: 'How does advertising work?' is that there are too many answers! Faced with this question the practitioner is not quite sure where to turn. How it works in terms of sales? How it works in terms of building an image? How it works for businesses? How it works for an individual consumer?

All of these represent possible, but partial answers. There is no grand theory or simple law. On the other hand, advertising does work – companies, their agencies and anyone who watches television knows that. Successful brands, from Levis to Lexus, from Kellogg's to Kit Kat stand as testament to its power. Yet the simple question goes unanswered – at least with a simple answer.

The truth is that there is no simple answer. Indeed, one could argue that the answer is different for every company that advertises. The logic here would be that because every brand is unique, every advertising solution and therefore its particular 'mechanism for effectiveness' is unique too.

There is in fact, something immensely powerful about the accumulation of evidence of advertising effectiveness derived in this way. And the UK leads the world in terms of the rigour with which that evidence has been collected.

For over 20 years, the IPA's Advertising Effectiveness Awards have rewarded those agency authors who have made the strongest cases for how advertising has changed the fortunes of an individual brand. The papers are extremely challenging to write, and are judged by some of the biggest names in the marketing industry: clients, agency heads, econometricians etc. To win, a demonstrable and watertight case has to be made – and then withstand an intellectual and logical 'pressure test' of major proportions!

The Databank created over those 20+ years now includes some 700 cases. But each is unique to its brand at a moment in time. And therein lies the problem. Of course, to an enlightened client or agency there are significant learnings to be had by analogy. Situations enjoyed by similar brands (especially if in a similar category) suggest parallels for today's brand.

But all too often, one hears the riposte (most often from clients): 'well, that may have worked for X, but why should it work for my brand?' or 'maybe that worked in 1990, but why should it still work today?' At worst, the whole of this outstanding body of knowledge can be set aside precisely *because* it is case-specific. In other words, the 'unique mechanism for effectiveness' argument gets taken to an extreme: 'my brand is unique, so what can I learn from what others have done?'

And that's why this book has been produced. Because while every brand and advertising campaign is unique, there are what might be called 'general proofs' of advertising effectiveness that underpin an awful lot of our industry's thinking. They are empirical, not just subjective, proofs – and they have wide applicability, beyond any one case or advertiser.

As a member of the IPA's 'Value of Advertising' committee, I was for some years charged with making the case for advertising to some pretty tough audiences: financial journalists, the City, analysts to name just three. What I found was that while individual advertising cases could be very powerful as illustrations, the real appetite from these audiences was for straightforward, understandable examples of general business effects.

And that is what I've set out to do here. This book is not really about advertising theory. It's about advertising facts. Empirical, demonstrable proofs of how advertising works for businesses. This is a new realm for many in the advertising industry. They would be the first to accept that financial proofs are the hardest to deliver. Indeed, most senior agency people never get to meet their clients' financial directors. Equally, some of the disciplines that might facilitate such a dialogue are themselves relatively new: shareholder value analysis, brand valuation, etc.

Agencies and client marketing directors seldom stray outside the 'comfort zone' of brands, image, personality and consumer effects in their day-to-day dialogue. Yet increasingly those marketing directors, and therefore their agencies, are being held accountable for the financial contribution of their advertising.

This book is here to help! It contains 20 chapters – most no longer than 2000 words, some considerably shorter – each of which addresses itself to a general proof of how advertising works. Each seeks to demonstrate in a pretty direct and to-the-point way how advertising contributes to businesses.

None of the chapters are case histories; all are intended to have potential applicability to *all* businesses.

The authors were briefed accordingly: keep the argument short and to the point, provide empirical evidence, distinguish between correlation and causality and, above all, think of who you're writing this chapter for.

This book is not aimed primarily at the advertising industry audience – though I'm sure they will find it useful. It is aimed at all of those people in *business* who use advertising to further their *business* goals.

The book is organised into four parts, according to where the advertising effect is to be seen:

- Company value effects
- Business performance effects
- Customer effects
- Brand effects

In addition, there is a brief introductory section and all the chapters are prefaced by a short executive summary describing 'the argument in brief'.

The individual authors are drawn from the advertising industry, the client community and the academic world – and their profiles are described briefly in the list of contributors. I'd like to take this opportunity to thank each of them for their contribution.

Finally, my thanks go to Hamish Pringle, Kezia Chapman and Jill Bentley – at the IPA, to my colleagues at Partners BDDH and to my PA, Nicki Jackson, for her help in putting everything together.

Leslie Butterfield

Contributors

Chris Baker

Chris is a past IPA Advertising Effectiveness Award Winner, and was also Convenor of Judges for the 1992 and 1994 IPA Advertising Effectiveness Awards and Editor of *Advertising Works* 7 and 8. He left the University of Sussex to join the British Market Research Bureau in 1973, moving to Saatchi & Saatchi as an Account Planner in 1981, becoming Deputy Head of Planning in 1988. He was a founder member and Planning Director of BST.BDDP in 1990, becoming Executive Planning Director of the merged BDDP.GGT in 1997, then joining TBWA as part of the subsequent merger in 1998. Chris is currently Director of Strategic Consultancy at TBWA\London, working with a range of local and international clients.

John Bartle

Until the end of 1999 John Bartle was the Joint Chief Executive of Bartle Bogle Hegarty (BBH), the advertising agency he co-founded in 1982. After graduating from Nottingham University with a degree in Industrial Economics he began his career in 1965 with Cadbury (later Cadbury Schweppes) and worked there for eight years, latterly as Marketing Services Manager for the company's Foods Group. He left in 1973 to become a co-founder of the London office of advertising agency TBWA. Initially Planning Director there, he was Joint Managing Director from 1979 until leaving to start BBH in 1982. He now has involvement with a number of organisations, in both the commercial and the voluntary sector, in non-executive/advisory capacities. These include COI Communications, the Guardian Media Group, the online media agency i-level, the digital production company Dare Digital and Barnardos. He was President of the IPA (Institute of Practitioners in Advertising) from 1995 to 1997, spent a number of years on the Council of the UK Advertising Association and is currently the President of NABS, the charity for the communications industry.

Marilyn Baxter

Marilyn Baxter is Chairman of the communications and brands research company Hall & Partners. Marilyn has spent over 25 years in advertising and research in a number of agencies, most notably at Saatchi and Saatchi where she was Executive Planning Director and Vice Chairman for 12 years. During her time in advertising she was a fellow and member of the Council of the Institute of Practitioners in Advertising and Chairman of the IPA's Value of Advertising Committee. Marilyn has also worked in a think tank (at IPC) and in public policy (at the National Economic Development Office). She is a frequent writer and speaker on advertising, communications and related issues.

Alexander L. Biel

A distinguished international research consultant, Alex Biel was educated at the University of Chicago and at Columbia. After service as associate director of research with Leo Burnett Chicago, he held a series of senior Ogilvy & Mather posts in Europe and North America. Until recently, he was executive director of WPP's Centre for Research and Development. He is a director (non-executive) of Research International and heads Alexander L. Biel & Associates, an international consulting firm based in Mill Valley, California.

Tim Broadbent

Tim is executive planning director, Bates UK. He is visiting professor of marketing of The London Institute, a Fellow of the IPA, and a member of the IPA Council and the IPA Value of Advertising Committee.

He is the only person to have twice won the Grand Prix in the IPA Advertising Effectiveness Awards, for John Smith's and BMW, and won a third Gold for Colgate. He was the convenor of judges of the IPA Awards in 2000 and editor of *Advertising Works 11*.

Tim graduated from Sussex University with a degree in philosophy and another in metaphysics. He has been an account planner since leaving Beecham to join BMP in 1978. He was a board director of FCB, Saatchi & Saatchi and WCRS, and planning director and managing partner of Y&R. He joined the new management team of Bates UK in 2000.

Stephan Buck

Stephan Buck is a main board non-executive director of Taylor Nelson Sofres plc (TNS), the largest UK market research company, and fourth largest worldwide. Having qualified as a mathematical statistician (PhD London University) he joined AGB (now part of the TNS Group) soon after its formation and was closely involved in its spectacular growth. In particular he helped to design, implement and run a number of innovative research services measuring consumers' media and purchasing habits in the UK and in many other countries abroad including the USA, Australasia and much of Europe. In 1987, Dr Buck introduced PeopleMeter technology to the US media industry and was one of the four nominees of the influential *Gallagher Report* as the 'one person who did the most for the progress of marketing and advertising in 1987'; the other nominees were the chairmen of Coca-Cola, The Ford Motor Company and P&G. Stephan Buck is a Fellow and an Honorary Member of the Market

Research Society, for which he is co-editor of its *Journal*. He is also on the editorial board of the *Journal of Brand Management*. He has served on the Council of the Royal Statistical Society and as a judge on the IPA Advertising Effectiveness Awards. Recognised as an expert commentator on marketing and the media, Dr Buck speaks frequently at conferences and has published many papers, some of which are considered to be standards in their field. Stephan is married with four children – all of whom pursue careers in research, advertising and marketing. He is a keen golfer and bridge player and once reached the UK final of the world poker championship – a triumph for probability theory!

Leslie Butterfield

Leslie Butterfield is one of the UK advertising industry's most respected strategists, and one of only a handful of people who shaped the discipline of Account Planning in the UK and now worldwide. But his first love was always brands and the marketing of them.

After completing a Masters Degree in Marketing, his advertising career began at Boase Massimi Pollitt (now BMP DDB) and from 1980 to 1987 he was Planning Director of Abbott Mead Vickers. In 1987, Leslie left to set up his own agency, Butterfield Day Devito Hockney. Now called Partners BDDH, the agency has gone from strength to strength over its 16-year history. He has been Planning Director and then Chairman of the agency since its inception.

Leslie has been a Fellow and Council Member of the IPA since 1992, and in 1997 he published *Excellence in Advertising*, a compilation of some of the outstanding papers delivered on IPA courses. A second edition was published in September 1999. Leslie also co-authored a book for the IPA entitled *Understanding the Financial Value of Brands*.

In March 2001, Leslie set up Butterfield8, a strategic brand consultancy within which Leslie is the anchor point for a team of 8 associates drawn from various business disciplines. Butterfield8 offers strategic brand advice to a number of clients including Mercedes-Benz, the Co-operative Group and the UK Government.

Simon Cole

Simon Cole is a Board Director of Interbrand and the Head of Interbrand's Brand Modelling practice. He is responsible for extending the core brand valuation product and developing its role as an active management tool for

brand owners and as a means to quantify the profit impact and effect of brand and marketing activity. He has been responsible for valuations of brands including American Express, Andersen Consulting, Accenture, Powergen, Heineken, TNT Post Group, and the BBC. Separate from this he has managed Brand Equity evaluations for major brands including Canon, Toyota and Gore Tex. Prior to joining Interbrand he was Business Planning Director at Saatchi & Saatchi where he was responsible for developing business, brand and communication strategy for a wide range of clients both in the UK and internationally. Simon has a BSc degree in Mathematics and a Masters degree in Operational Research, both from the University of Sussex.

Will Collin

After graduating from Keble College, Oxford, Will began his career at BMP DDB as a trainee account planner in 1989. Over the following eight years he worked on a range of accounts, including Heinz Baked Beans, Alliance & Leicester and Sony. In 1994, he was a founding member of BMP Interaction, the agency's specialist interactive and digital unit, where he was closely involved in early interactive TV trials with Cambridge Cable and BT. He was promoted to the agency board in 1996. In 1997 he moved to media specialists New PHD as communications strategy director, with a brief to bring the consumer-focused disciplines of account planning to the world of media strategy. Working on accounts such as BT, Mercedes-Benz, NCR, BBC and UKTV, Will developed the agency's strategic thinking and its use of qualitative research in media strategy. In 2000 he founded Naked Communications with fellow New PHD Group directors Jon Wilkins and John Harlow. Naked was awarded Campaign of the Year for its work on Selfridges in the *Campaign* Media Awards in 2001, and was named Agency of the Year by *Media Week* in 2002. Will's current clients include Hutchison 3G UK, the Department of Health and Sony PlayStation. He has been a regular speaker on New Media for (among others) the Media Circle, The Marketing Council and The Account Planning Group, and he was also a judge in the Direct Mail category at the 2002 D&AD Awards.

Andrew Crosthwaite

Andrew Crosthwaite read English at Worcester College, Oxford before joining Ogilvy Benson and Mather as a graduate trainee in Account Management. After spells at Publicis and Doyle Dane Bernbach, he joined FCO as Planning Director in 1985. In 1993 FCO merged as one of the constituents of Euro RSCG Wnek Gosper, where he became Head of Planning. In 1996 Andrew set up a new venture under the Euro RSCG corporate umbrella called Euro RSCG Upstream, a brand and communications consultancy working with clients inside and outside the advertising agency's roster. At the beginning of 1999 he left to set up an independent brand consultancy. He is a Fellow of the IPA and a member of The Marketing Society's Innovations Team. He won a bronze in the 1994 IPA Effectiveness Awards and a Commendation in 1996.

Charlie Dobres

Charlie Dobres is CEO, i-level. He has been working in new media since the beginning of 1995. In 1996, he created Lowe Digital, an autonomous digital marketing operation. This specialist division of ad agency Lowe Howard-Spink rapidly became established as one of the UK's leading exponents of digital marketing.

Charlie was a founder member of the Digital Marketing Group, an association of the UK's leading ad agencies with new media operations. After this he went on to become the founding general secretary of the Interactive Advertising Bureau (UK).

Then, at the end of 1998, he became one of the co-founders of i-level, now the UK's leading online media agency. i-level represents major advertisers such as BT, Smile, Yell and William Hill, and has been both *Revolution* and *Campaign* magazine's Digital Media Agency of the Year for the last two years. Aside from online advertising, i-level has now expanded into digital marketing consultancy and website efficiency auditing.

Charlie lives in Pinner with wife Karen and daughter Millicent-Muriel.

Peter Field

Peter Field began his career in 1982 at BMP where he trained as a planner. He spent 9 years at AMV.BBDO before moving on to manage the Planning departments of Dorlands and Grey. Since 1997 he has been an independent planning consultant as well as more recently a partner in Eatbigfish, the challenger brand consultancy. He was a member of the IPA Value of Advertising Committee for five years and head of the IPA Data Bank of effectiveness case histories.

James R. Gregory

Jim Gregory is founder and CEO of Corporate Branding, LLC, a global brand strategy and communications firm based in Stamford, Connecticut with offices in New York and Tokyo. With 30 years of experience in advertising and branding, Jim is recognized as a leading expert on brand management and credited with developing pioneering and innovative tools for measuring the power of brands and their impact on a corporation's financial performance.

Among the tools Jim has developed is the Corporate Branding Index® (CBI); a research vehicle that has tracked the reputation and financial performance of over 1000 publicly traded companies in 45 industries since 1990. CoreBrand uses the CBI to help clients understand how their brand compares with industry peers and determine how communications can impact corporate reputation and financial performance – including stock price.

Jim serves on the brand council of the New York Stock Exchange and is a frequent speaker on the financial benefits of advertising and brand management for *The Wall Street Journal* as well as *Business Week*.

Jim has written four books on creating value with brands, *Marketing Corporate Image*, *Leveraging the Corporate Brand*, *Branding Across Borders*, and his latest book, *The Best of Branding*.

Mr Gregory may be reached directly at 203.564.2439 or jgregory@corebrand.com.

Johnny Hornby

Johnny Hornby graduated from Edinburgh University to become an Ogilvy & Mather trainee. He went to CDP as Board Account Director in 1995, and became a 'face to watch' in Campaign. He left his position as Client Services Director at CDP to become Group Account Director at TBWA in 1998. He was appointed Joint Managing Director of TBWA in 2000 and was responsible for winning and running the campaign that saw Labour to a second landslide victory in 2001. In July 2001 he and Simon Clemmow joined Charles Inge to form Clemmow Hornby Inge, the agency now has clients including Tango, Heineken, *The Telegraph* and Carphone Warehouse.

John Philip Jones

John is an American advertising professor born in Britain. He has 27 years' professional experience, including 25 years in international operations with the J. Walter Thompson Company, and 21 years at the Newhouse School of Public Communications, Syracuse University, New York. John is adjunct professor at the Royal Melbourne Institute of Technology, Australia and author of five books (translated into six foreign languages) and more than seventy articles in major journals, both professional and general. He is editor and part-author of

five major handbooks covering all aspects of professional advertising practice, published by Sage Publications Inc. Employed as consultant by numerous first-rank national and international organisations, mainly advertisers and advertising agencies, John travels all over the world in connection with this work. He is a specialist in the measurement and evaluation of advertising effects and originator of two widely-used concepts to measure them. John has been the recipient of a number of national awards and recognitions. A new book *Fables, Fashions and Facts About Advertising: A Study of 35 Enduring Myths*, will be published in 2003.

Stephen King

Stephen spent most of his working life at J. Walter Thompson in London and became a director of the worldwide company in 1985. He worked on many of the agency's major accounts, and was involved in marketing, advertising research, new product development, market modelling and computer groups. In 1968 he established JWT's Account Planning department, the first in UK advertising. From the mid-1980s he concentrated on establishing common advertising planning methods for the agency worldwide. After retiring from JWT in 1988 he worked for four years as a non-executive director of WPP, and did freelance consultancy work for American Express, De Beers, Shell, Nestlé, HongKong Telecom, JWT and Hill & Knowlton, and from 1992 to 2001 was a non-executive director of the Henley Centre. He is author of *Developing New Brands* and many articles on branding, advertising and market research; and has been Visiting Professor of Marketing Communications at the Cranfield School of Management.

Hamish Pringle

Hamish graduated from Trinity College, Oxford, in 1973, with a degree in PPE and joined Ogilvy & Mather as a graduate trainee in 1973. After spells at Boase Massimi Pollitt, Publicis, Abbott Mead Vickers, his own agency Madell Wilmot Pringle, and Leagas Delaney, Hamish joined KHBB in 1992 and became Chairman & CEO in 1995. Following the merger in 1997, he became Vice-Chairman, and Director of Marketing of Saatchi &

Saatchi. During this period Hamish had a variety of involvements with the IPA. These included being a member of the IPA President's Committee (1994–96), a Council member (1985–86, 1989–98), Chairman of the IPA Advertising Effectiveness Committee (1993–96) and IPA Society Chairman (1984–85). He was also Chairman of the NABS the industry charity (1996–98) and served on the NABS General Management Committee (1993–2000). He has co-authored two books – *Brand Spirit* (1999) and *Brand Manners* (2001). In August 2001 Hamish became Director General of the IPA (see www.ipa.co.uk).

Malcolm White

Having graduated from London University, with an MA in English Language and Literature, Malcolm started his advertising career at DMB&B. Moving on to BMP DDB Needham, he worked on a broad range of clients including Crookes Healthcare (OTC Pharmaceuticals), Trebor Bassett, COI/Department of Social Security, and was appointed to the board of the agency. At BMP,

Malcolm was the strategy director for the Labour Party during the successful general election campaign in 1997. In his own right, Malcolm has won an IPA Effectiveness Award for Strepsils (while at BMP) and an APG award for Nestlé Rowntree (while at APL). Malcolm joined Partners BDDH in 1998 with a brief to develop the agency's creative thinking mission, and he is responsible for the agency's planning department. Since then they have won two IPA Effectiveness Awards for their work on Co-op Retail and both a Gold and the Grand Prix at the 2001 APG Awards for their work on Transport for London.

Introduction: The value of advertising . . . and brands

Leslie Butterfield

Advertising comes and goes, but brands live on. And that's because it is brands rather than just their advertising that deliver sustainable long-term value to clients' businesses. 'Sustainable' because they can command loyalty. 'Long-term' because one is talking often about decades of contribution. And 'value' because, brands *are* valuable – to marketing companies, and therefore to agencies.

If anyone is in any doubt about the value of brands they need only do two things. Firstly, look at the extent to which the market capitalisation of branded goods companies exceeds their tangible asset value. For the whole US stock market this figure has grown from around +50 per cent in 1993 to around +90 per cent in 2001. In the case of a company like Coca-Cola, for example, the figure can be as high as +3000 per cent! In the UK, three examples will suffice: for Cadbury Schweppes the excess of market capitalisation over tangibles totals some £1.0bn (+22 per cent), for Sainsbury's it's £1.4bn (+40 per cent) and for Scottish and Newcastle Breweries a whopping £2.4bn (+110 per cent)!

Secondly, look at what acquisitive companies are prepared to pay for brands. In the United States, Philip Morris paid £8bn for Kraft, four times its book value as a business. In the UK, Nestlé paid £2.8bn for Rowntree, five times its book value, for brands that included Kit Kat and Polo, both of which have subsequently been exploited and exported to their fuller potential.

Brands therefore are increasingly being recognised as critically important to many major corporations. Former Unilever chairman Sir Michael Perry summed this up almost perfectly when he said:

> The major assets of a consumer business, overwhelmingly, are its brands. They are of incalculable value, representing both its heritage and its future. To succeed as a consumer products business there is no alternative but to invent, nurture and invest in brands.

That last point about investment is particularly interesting to those who work in advertising. Because, seen in this way, brands are assets in which one invests – rather than, as at present, marketing 'items' against which costs are allocated, and accounted for only in the year in which they arise.

In parallel with the upsurge of interest in brands, there has also been a growing interest in the whole issue of brand valuation. This subject has been elevated from a rather arcane discussion about balance sheet accounting to a much more fundamental position of importance. Brand valuation allows marketing companies to quantify the actual financial value of their most prized assets. No longer need that value be, as Sir Michael says, incalculable.

None of this may be any great revelation to the reader. Most will not need convincing of the part that brands can play in delivering sustainable long-term value. The real questions are: 'Do others appreciate this?' and, 'Is the advertising contribution to this value recognised?' At the moment, I suspect the answers here would be 'partially' and 'sometimes'.

Taking the first question, the IPA in conjunction with KPMG recently commissioned a survey of finance directors' attitudes to marketing and advertising. The findings from that survey were highly revealing. In answer to the question, 'To what degree do you see the following as a necessary investment to long-term growth?' marketing came fifth out of five. But when it comes to cutting budgets when costs are under pressure, marketing and advertising are first. This is hardly surprising though when one realises that the criteria that most FDs use to measure marketing and advertising effectiveness are pretty blunt. Sales volume is rated more than four times as important as brand image, for example, in making those judgements.

And as to the other question, about recognition of the advertising contribution, Dominic Cadbury, Chairman of Cadbury Schweppes, was quoted in *Marketing Week* as saying:

> A fixation with advertising makes it unsurprising that marketing has a struggle to be taken seriously in the boardroom and that the notion of marketing as a source of competitive advantage is regarded with suspicion.

What a pity that such an eminent commentator should take such a dim view of the marketing and advertising contribution. In response to a letter from myself though, he substantiated his view as follows:

> I am committed to the importance of marketing in all its aspects as I am to improving the effectiveness of what we do. However, [he continues] I do think there is a growing issue around our accountability to our shareholders because I see them becoming more active in analysing and questioning marketing expenditures.

It is these twin issues of effectiveness and accountability that sit at the heart of the debate about the advertising contribution, and it is they too that are central to just about every chapter in this book.

The IPA is at the forefront of trying to promote a greater understanding of the financial value attributable to brands as a key measure of advertising effectiveness. For too long, the focus in the advertising industry has been on short-term advertising effects on sales and share and not enough on the harder-to-quantify effects on brand or even company value.

The IPA has already sought to broaden the criteria by which the Advertising Effectiveness Awards are judged to take account of this expanded definition of advertising's role. Its mission now is to try to elevate the debate, by demonstrating that the financial value of a brand can also be a key measure of advertising effectiveness and that this automatically brings a whole new slant to marketing and advertising budget decisions. Even if only used as an internal tool, to get all disciplines within a branded business to focus on the asset value of their brands, this in turn might lead to those other disciplines viewing advertising expenditures as investment rather than just costs.

In the future, it will only be by having evidence like this that marketers (and their agencies) will be able to make a sustainable case to other disciplines within their companies for investment in brands. Marketing departments, and agencies in particular, need to raise their sights as well as their standards if they are to have a seat at the table when these sort of decisions are being made.

The IPA believes it is right that agencies should take responsibility for the effectiveness of their work for a client – effectiveness in all senses including financial accountability. The ultimate contribution an agency can make is enhancing the shareholder value of its client's business.

As the reader moves through this book, he or she will find other examples of this kind of thinking. New ways of looking at how advertising's financial effectiveness can be measured. New approaches to assessing the accountability of advertising expenditures. New ways of understanding, in other words, the full scope of the advertising contribution. And in so doing, the hope is that we can start to build bridges between the advertising industry, on the one hand, and the marketing, financial and management communities within client companies, on the other.

Finally, the reader will have already noticed that at all points I have used the single word 'advertising' as the focus of our interest. In today's world, it is increasingly clear and recognised that 'traditional' advertising is but one tool in the box marked 'marketing communications'. Other tools in that box include direct marketing, sales promotion, sponsorship, PR, digital media, etc.

The fact remains, however, that, outside the marketing communications industry, the common vernacular *is* 'advertising' – and the word is often used as both a shorthand and 'catch-all' for those other marketing communication tools. Since the primary audience for this book is indeed those outside the industry, I have used the word advertising pretty much throughout.

Indeed, even within the portfolio of marketing communications, advertising does still have a unique part to play. None of the other tools, in my opinion, quite shares its ability to dramatise, excite, stir the emotions or reach into both the hearts and minds of an audience. That's why it has sometimes been described as the last great source of unfair competitive advantage! That's why its unique contribution is worth studying. And that's why this book has been produced.

PART A

Company Value Effects

The argument in brief: Chapter 1

New evidence from the PIMS database commissioned by the IPA proves that:

Advertising impacts on profitability because it helps determine customer value

- The correlation between advertising and profitability is not direct but indirect.
- It is customer value which drives profitability.
- And advertising contributes to perceived customer value.

Advertising has a direct effect on perceived quality – perceived quality determines customer value

- There is a direct correlation between advertising and perceived quality.
- Successful advertising also builds product/service image and company reputation which are key components of perceived quality.
- Perceived quality drives customer value.

Successful advertising spends heavily relative to its share of the market

- Those brands or businesses which invest in advertising to produce a share of voice over and above their share of market outperform their competition.

Advertising which not only outspends relative to its share of the market, but also succeeds in building quality perceptions of the product, is the most successful of all

- The PIMS database clearly shows that the style and content of advertising has a significant impact on how successful it is. Spend alone cannot determine success.
- Advertising which focuses on product image, company reputation and/or other key attributes that drive customers' perceptions of relative quality, and hence value, will be successful in business terms.

Chapter 1

How advertising impacts on profitability

Leslie Butterfield

Introducing PIMS

Tom Peters, the celebrated management consultant, describes PIMS as being 'the world's most extensive strategic information database'. From its genesis at Harvard in 1972, it now encompasses data on over 3000 companies – totalling a massive 20 000 years of business experience. The appendix to this chapter covers the details of the construction of the database, and the nature of the information that is collected. Suffice to say here that the focus for this study was the 200+ companies operating principally in branded consumer products in Europe (see Figure 1.1).

The IPA quest

The IPA's interest in the PIMS database stems from an awareness of the growing demand from senior management for 'general proofs' of the value of advertising, to set alongside the expanding databank of individual case studies of advertising effectiveness that the IPA has assembled over the last 18 years.

Among these general proofs are the long-term studies conducted by, among others, AC Nielsen, on the negative effect on brand share of the removal of advertising support, work in the USA by the American Association of

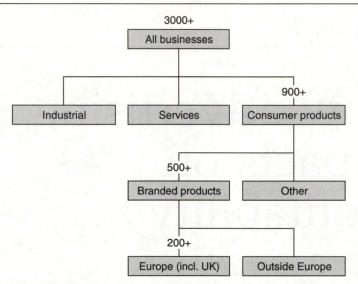

Figure I.I Selecting comparisons from the PIMS database. (*Source*: PIMS database © 1998 PIMS Europe Ltd)

Advertising Agencies on the impact of advertising on stock price performance, and work by a number of academics over the last two recessions to identify the long-term effects of significant decreases in promotional support for brands.

In addition to these, the IPA has been active in promoting the issue of Brand Valuation – as a means by which marketing companies and their agencies can understand better the considerable intangible value of their branded assets – and invest in them accordingly.

The relationship between advertising and profitability

The analysis described here, by contrast, focuses specifically on the relationship between advertising and profitability* – both directly and, perhaps more importantly, indirectly, via the medium of perceived quality. The importance of perceived quality to brand buying decisions and loyalty is hard to overstate. David Aaker in his excellent book *Building Successful Brands* describes the power of the relationship fully, and concludes:

---

*Defined for the purposes of this paper as Return on Investment (ROI).

> Perceived quality is the single most important contributor to a company's return on investment (ROI), having more impact than market share, R&D or marketing expenditures...[it] is usually at the heart of what customers are buying, and in that sense, it is a bottom-line measure of the impact of a brand identity. More interesting, though, perceived quality reflects a measure of 'goodness' that spreads over all elements of the brand...When perceived quality improves, so generally do other elements of customers' perception of the brand.

Our quest here therefore was to explore the quantitative *and causal* relationship between advertising, perceived quality and profitability. And like most quests, ours was not a simple journey.

The PIMS model

Figure 1.2 illustrates the well-established causal relationships that we know to exist within the main PIMS database. PIMS are unequivocal that, on the basis of the *whole* sample of 3000+ businesses, providing a superior value offering to customers (whether that be trade customers or consumers of branded products) is a prime driver of growth and profitability. Furthermore, within our sub-sample of branded consumer products, we can show that relative Customer Value is highly correlated with profitability (see Figure 1.3).

Defining customer value

Customer Value in turn is defined from the customer's perspective as a combination of quality of total offering, and price, both of these being measured *relative* to competitors. Of these two, given the strength of David Aaker's argument above (and indeed from PIMS' own evidence) it is relative perceived quality that is of most interest to us. Hence our need for an analysis that

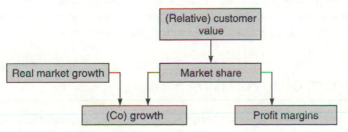

Figure 1.2 Links from customer value to profitability and growth. (*Source*: PIMS database © 1998 PIMS Europe Ltd)

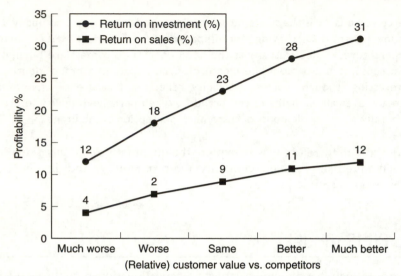

Figure 1.3 Customer value drives profitability. (*Source*: PIMS database © 1998 PIMS Europe Ltd)

would allow us to examine the direct and causal relationship between advertising and profitability via the intermediate variable of relative perceived quality. Finally, we also knew that one of the principal *components* of relative quality is 'product image and company reputation' (see Figure 1.4).

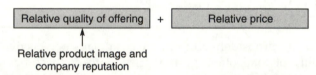

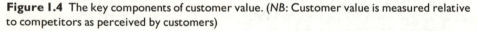

Figure 1.4 The key components of customer value. (*NB*: Customer value is measured relative to competitors as perceived by customers)

Armed with these numerous linkages and relationships, we now went on to examine the extent to which we could demonstrate the role that advertising spend can play in shaping and influencing the above factors.

The impact of advertising

Our first special analysis was designed to examine the relationship between absolute levels of advertising spend (expressed as a % of sales) and relative quality of offering, and the findings are shown in Figure 1.5. Superficially the

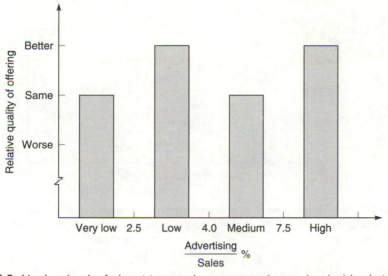

Figure 1.5 Absolute levels of advertising spend are *not* strongly correlated with relative quality of offering. (*Source:* PIMS database of European consumer goods businesses © 1998 PIMS Europe Ltd)

results look disappointing: there is little correlation between absolute levels of advertising spend and relative quality of offering.

The importance of relative spend

Spirits rose considerably though when we repeated the analysis, but this time looking at advertising spend (again expressed in A:S terms) relative to competitors... effectively a measure of 'share of voice' relative to share of market. Figure 1.6 shows the findings from this analysis and the result is clear: advertising spend *relative to competitors* is strongly correlated with relative quality of offering.

The conclusion here is clear and important. Namely that in influencing customer perceptions of the quality of your product (and hence its value) it is not a question of how *much* you spend, but of how much you *out*spend your competitors. Two further points are worth noting here.

Because there is no correlation in the analysis in Figure 1.5, paradoxically this gives us *more* confidence in the causality of the relationship described in Figure 1.6. If the reverse causality were true (i.e. that better quality led to higher adspend) then we would expect the same relationship to be reflected in the absolute spends in Figure 1.5 as in the relative spends at Figure 1.6. As this is not the case our confidence in the *true* causality of Figure 1.6 increases.

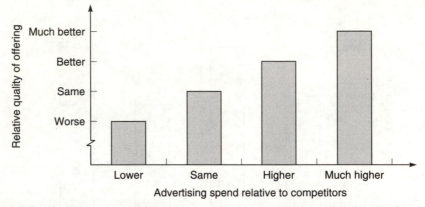

Figure 1.6 Advertising spend *relative to competitors** is strongly correlated with relative quality of offering. (*Source*: PIMS database of European consumer goods businesses © 1998 PIMS Europe Ltd)

The point about outspending competitors should not be taken as a 'counsel of despair' by No. 2 brands and below! What we are saying here is that those brands need to outspend (in share of voice terms) *relative to their share of market* – not absolutely more than (e.g.) the brand leader.

Advertising and perceived quality

This same logic held true when we went on to examine a key component of perceived quality: product image and company reputation. Again the analysis showed little evidence of correlation between *absolute* spends and this component. But when we examined our relative spend measure (i.e. share of voice) the correlation was powerful (see Figure 1.7). It is this analysis that leads to our second key conclusion from this study.

Because 'product image and company reputation' is both a component of quality and *a driver of it*, we would suggest that it is not just 'any old advertising' that matters, but rather advertising that seeks and succeeds in building quality perceptions of the product, either directly or through the intermediary of product image and company reputation.

---

*This is a comparison of the advertising to sales ratios of a business and its main competitors:
Lower – Advertising/sales ratios of its main competitors are at least 1% point more than this business.
Same – Advertising/sales ratio of this business is between 1% point less and 1% point more than its main competitors.
Higher – Advertising/sales ratio of this business is 1–3% points more than its main competitors.
Much Higher – Advertising/sales ratio of this business is at least 3% points more than its competitors.

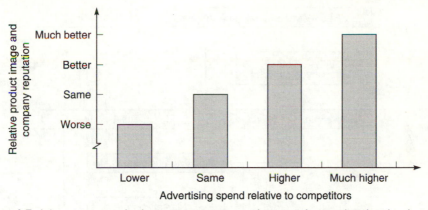

Figure 1.7 Advertising spend *relative to competitors* is also strongly correlated with relative product image and company reputation. (*Source*: PIMS database of European consumer goods businesses © 1998 PIMS Europe Ltd)

How advertising impacts on profitability

The combination of these two special analyses, and the conclusions that stem from them, mean that we can now extend the model that we first examined in Figure 1.2. Figure 1.8 shows that extended model – with the top three levels having been added as a result of the analyses reported here. Furthermore we can be very confident about the causality (and not just the correlation) of each of the individual linkages illustrated.

Conclusions

While it would have been delightful to have shown a simple causal relationship between advertising and profitability, the real-world influence of other factors means that we have had to demonstrate causality through a set of intervening variables. Of these, by far the most important is relative customer value – and we are able to demonstrate the impact of advertising on this variable through its effect on relative perceived quality. Importantly though, we have seen that it is relative (rather than absolute) advertising spend levels that show a strong correlation here. This leads to the interesting conclusion that it is not how much you spend, but how much you outspend competitors that matters.

The data also suggests a second conclusion: that the nature of the advertising matters too – its focus should be on product image, company reputation and/or other key attributes that drive customers' perceptions of relative quality and hence value. The linkages thus arrived at (summarised in Figure 1.8) are more

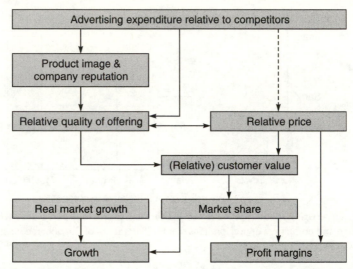

Figure 1.8 Links from advertising to profitability and growth. (*Source*: PIMS database © 1998 PIMS Europe Ltd)

complex than we might have wished for ideally but they do at least have a 'real-world' feel to them.

The analysis described here does not suggest that all advertising leads to increased profitability (i.e. that there is a universal relationship here); it suggests strongly though that advertising that builds quality *does* have just that effect. Rarely are causal relationships easy to demonstrate in areas such as advertising. At least, though, with this analysis we can have confidence in the ultimate effect of advertising on corporate fortunes. And while the linkages we have been able to demonstrate are less simple than most models of advertising effect, they may be more honest than some!

Appendix: The PIMS database explained

The PIMS database of business unit performance captures structural characteristics and competitive and financial performance of business units in international firms. The name 'PIMS' – (the) Profit Impact of Market Strategy – describes the essential purpose of building and using the PIMS database: namely, to identify and quantify how non-financial factors, especially market strategy of businesses, impact both on their profitability and other measures of performance.

By 1997, there were more than 3000 businesses in the PIMS database. Each business is a strategic unit in a company, delivering a specific set of products and services to specific customers against specific competitors. There are businesses from all parts of the world although the majority are in the North American Free Trade Area or Europe. Each business unit is described quantitatively in terms of:

- Characteristics of the market which the business serves
- The competitive position of the business in that market
- Profits, cost structure, capital employed and productivity

This data captures at least four consecutive years of information on how each business has actually performed. Businesses contained in the PIMS database represent a wide spectrum of industry sectors. For this IPA paper, a relevant sub-set of businesses was selected for analysis. Of some 900 consumer goods businesses, approximately 500 are branded products businesses of which more than 200 are located in Europe.

The profile of each business is captured through over 400 variables, supplied by managers of the business units concerned and verified by PIMS staff. All data is supplied in confidence in the course of strategic evaluation assignments, so there is a real incentive for managers to supply accurate data (checked by PIMS consultants) for appropriate comparison against analogous businesses in the PIMS database.

The PIMS database was originally designed at General Electric and Harvard Business School in the early 1970s and later by the Strategic Planning Institute in Boston, USA to enable statistical analysis of differences in performance between businesses in different competitive circumstances and different industries, and to identify and quantify underlying performance 'drivers'.

For more details about the contents and history of the PIMS database, see *The PIMS Principles* by R. Buzzell and B. Gale (Free Press, 1987).

The argument in brief: Chapter 2

Research from Corporate Branding, LLC Stamford, Connecticut, USA argues the case that advertising has an impact on share price because:

- Corporate brand image is a combination of familiarity and favourability.
- Corporate brand image impacts both on business results and the way the stock market evaluates a company in terms of price/earnings ratio and the cash flow multiple.
- Image has a direct influence on 5 per cent of the variation in stock price.
- Image has an indirect influence on 70 per cent of the other factors explaining stock price.
- Advertising is the single biggest contributor to image.

Chapter 2

How advertising impacts on share price

James Gregory
With a UK perspective from Jeremy Hicks

About the research

Our research focused on 50 *Fortune* 100 companies over a seven-year period, measuring reputation changes in relation to advertising-spending patterns, earnings growth, revenue, and stock performance. In the next phase of our research, we enlarged our base to 220 companies to expand and further quantify the knowledge gained from the first analysis. Analysis on this larger scale was completely consistent with our original findings. In fact, we were able to quantify our image and stock-price models in even greater detail.

The relationships linking corporate brand communications, corporate image and shareholder value

Figure 2.1 demonstrates the chain of events that link corporate brand communications, corporate image, and shareholder value. The core of the equation is corporate brand communications, which is corporate, brand, and trade advertising carrying the corporate name, and which has quantitatively been shown to

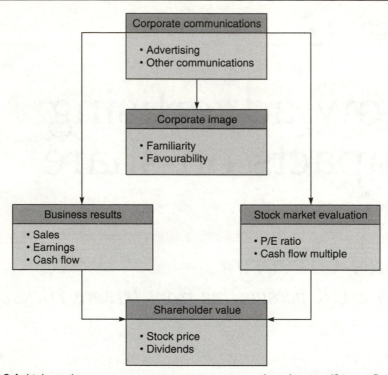

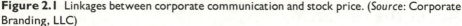

Figure 2.1 Linkages between corporate communication and stock price. (*Source*: Corporate Branding, LLC)

impact corporate image. Corporate image, in turn, has two dimensions. Image is a combination of familiarity and favourability. Familiarity is a quantitative measure of the number of business decision makers familiar with the company – its audience. Favourability is the qualitative aspect of image: how do those people who are familiar with the company see it? How do business decision makers view the company's reputation, its management, and its investment potential?

CB's research discovered that corporate brand image impacts in two ways. One is in business results: the sales generated, and the earnings and cash flow that come from those sales. Findings demonstrate that image also affects the way the stock market evaluates the company in terms of the price/earnings ratio (the premium the market puts on earnings when setting stock price) and the cash flow multiple (the premium put on cash flow).

Along this chain of events, the cash flow multiple is affected both by image and business results. A fast-growing company like Microsoft is a good example of how business results impact its multiple. Because the stock market is concerned with tomorrow as well as today, it responds to a company growing into the future, a company that will show more earnings longer term. A fast-growing company typically has a high price/earnings ratio and cash flow multiple.

Business results and stock-market evaluation in turn influence shareholder value. Shareholder value is a combination of growth in the stock price and the dividends paid. The dividends are affected by the sales, earnings and cash flow from business results, and not stock market evaluation. The stock price, however, is influenced by both the business results and the stock market evaluation.

How much does image impact stock price?

The factors that impact stock price, based on this research, are illustrated by Figure 2.2 CB's analysis explains 87 per cent of the variance in stock price (a mathematical definition of the variation in stock price from company to company) by a number of factors, most of which are business related. Not surprisingly, cash flow, earnings and dividends explain 30 per cent of the variance in stock price. If a company's cash flow is high, earnings are high, and dividends are high, the company will usually enjoy a higher stock price.

Cash flow, earnings and dividends tend to form a base that the market builds on. Other characteristics of the company grow from that base. Stock price growth explains 20 per cent of the variance in stock price. If the stock has been growing steadily for the past few years, chances are it will continue to

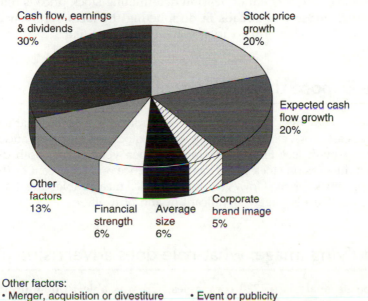

Other factors:
• Merger, acquisition or divestiture   • Event or publicity
• New product or process   • Financial advisor recommendations
• Recent industry/market trends   • Management changes

Figure 2.2 Factors explaining stock price. (*Source*: Corporate Branding, LLC)

do so, and the stock market accords it a premium. Another 20 per cent piece of the pie is expected cash flow growth. Expected cash flow growth is determined by how analysts expect cash flow to grow in the future.

An interesting factor that came out in the research is company size. It is best to be an average-sized company. This factor accounts for 6 per cent of the pie. Companies that are either very small or very big carry a real disadvantage in terms of stock market valuation.

All other things being equal, medium-sized companies tend to be valued more highly than either small or large companies by the stock market. It's more difficult for a huge company like General Motors to grow fast. Obviously, the disadvantage of being so large can be outweighed by other positive factors, so that the drawback of large size is overcome. The same would hold true for smaller-than-average companies. Smaller companies could be perceived to lack the resources or staying power of a large company. However, other positive factors might outweigh the disadvantages.

CB's research has shown that image explains 5 per cent of the variation in stock price. Image is not a huge percentage when you compare it to cash flow, earnings or dividends, but it is definitely significant, and an exciting and important find. Amid other business-related factors that a company has little control over, image is a real leverage factor, a tool that can be used to affect a company's stock price. And the fact that it is very nearly as important a factor as the 6 per cent explained by financial strength (a company's soundness based on stable earnings and amount of debt) in determining stock price is remarkable. This research made real inroads in deciphering the factors influencing stock price, with 87 per cent of the variance positively identified.

Image is more than the sum of its parts

In addition to having a direct impact on stock price, it is certain that image also influences cash flow, earnings and dividends, stock price growth and expected cash flow growth (see Figure 2.3). Image, when you add up both direct and indirect influences on stock price, has an influence on 75 per cent of the factors explaining stock price. However, the specific, measurable direct impact of image (5 per cent) is hugely significant in and of itself.

Quantifying image: what role does advertising play?

Based on its analysis of 220 companies, CB was able to quantify the most significant factors explaining corporate brand image (Figure 2.4). The lion's share of image can be attributed to advertising spending, weighing in at a hefty 30 per cent, the most important factor in determining image. Company

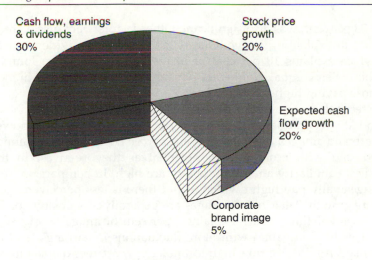

Cash flow, earnings & dividends 30%

Stock price growth 20%

Expected cash flow growth 20%

Corporate brand image 5%

Of the factors explaining stock price:
- Corporate brand image has a 5 per cent direct impact
- 70 per cent of other factors are influenced by corporate brand image

Figure 2.3 Factors influenced by corporate brand image. (*Source*: Corporate Branding, LLC)

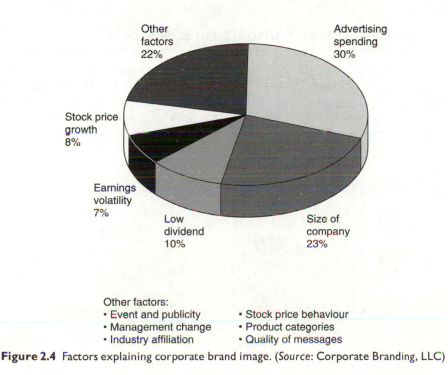

Other factors 22%

Advertising spending 30%

Stock price growth 8%

Earnings volatility 7%

Low dividend 10%

Size of company 23%

Other factors:
- Event and publicity
- Management change
- Industry affiliation
- Stock price behaviour
- Product categories
- Quality of messages

Figure 2.4 Factors explaining corporate brand image. (*Source*: Corporate Branding, LLC)

size, at 23 per cent, was also significant. Other factors were discovered that are important in explaining image. One is the amount of dividends a company pays, which explains 10 per cent of image. Interestingly, we found that, all other things being equal, companies paying low dividends have higher images than those paying higher dividends.

The technology category provides two good examples of this phenomenon: Intel and Microsoft. Both pay relatively low dividends, but have powerful and positive brand images because they are perceived as more dynamic, future-oriented, and with more growth potential as they re-invest in their own companies. Familiarity and favourability are high. In comparison, the electric utilities generally pay high dividends, but there is less perceived opportunity for future growth. Their brand images are generally less positive or powerful.

Earnings volatility, which explains 7 per cent of image, works similarly to low dividends. Companies with more fluctuations in earnings tend to have a better image. Again, as a rule, high-technology companies display more market volatility than the utilities.

The last significant factor contributing to image is stock price growth itself, which explains 5 per cent of image. A stock showing growth in the past will have a better image than a stock that has not been growing. As its analysis expanded, CB was able to explain 78 per cent of the variance in image.

The range of image's impact on stock price

Figure 2.5 demonstrates the percentage of variance explained by image. The average is 5 per cent. But for 25 per cent of the companies in the high-growth range, it is actually higher than that. Image plays a more significant role in a fast-growing or quickly changing industry. In other words, image will work harder to impact a higher stock price. Lucent Technologies, for example, has

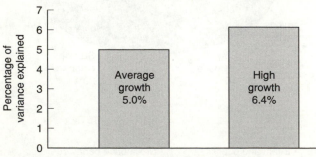

Figure 2.5 Percentage of variance explained by corporate brand image. (*Source*: Corporate Branding, LLC)

more leverage to raise its image than a utility, or a more average growth company, like DuPont. High-growth companies like Lucent tend to get more leverage from their advertising dollars than low-growth companies.

The varying benefits of advertising on shareholder value

The distribution of benefit/cost ratio is the increased shareholder value divided by the cost of advertising, across the 220 companies studied in the research. Based on the quantified relationships between advertising and image, and image and stock price, CB was able to estimate how different levels of advertising spending would affect stock price and, therefore, shareholder value (stock price multiplied by the number of shares outstanding). A benefit/cost ratio can then be developed for each company.

Figure 2.6 shows the distribution of benefit/cost ratios. If your company falls in the range of a benefit/cost ratio of less than one (29 per cent of sample companies), you should be advertising based on your company's business needs, since you cannot justify spending on the basis of increased shareholder value alone. With a benefit/cost ratio of between one and two (21 per cent of the sample companies), your company would be better off to advertise than not, but a shortage of cash or extraordinary investment opportunities may preclude advertising investment.

In the two to four range (24 per cent of the sample companies), an excellent opportunity to advertise exists based only on increasing shareholder value.

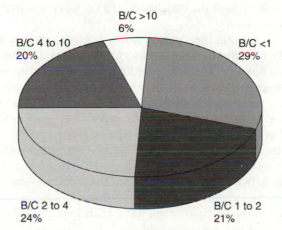

Figure 2.6 Distribution of benefit/cost ratios. (*Source*: Corporate Branding, LLC)

Your company would be hard pressed to find investment opportunities that show better results. If your company's benefit/cost ratio reaches above four (20 per cent of the sample companies), you have a tremendous amount of leverage in using corporate advertising to impact image and, in turn, stock price. Amplify that for the 6 per cent of companies in the range above 10. The research even identified a very few fortunate companies with a benefit/cost ratio of more than 20.

Knowing where your company stands in terms of this benefit/cost ratio is extremely valuable information in helping to set communications strategies, information your CEO and CFO will want to know.

A UK perspective

By Jeremy Hicks, Group Finance Director, Abbott Mead Vickers.BBDO in the run-up to the acquisition by Omnicom

The UK is widely perceived as being culturally similar to the USA, at least in a business sense. In both markets advertising and marketing are well-developed industries; the population of both countries is made up of sophisticated and media literate consumers. The two countries' stock markets represent variations on the same 'Anglo-Saxon' corporate/capitalist model.

Such differences as there are between the two are relatively insignificant compared with the similarities. Compare the UK with some other European cultures and this reality is emphasised. Compare the UK or the USA with some eastern economies (the former Iron Curtain countries, China) or southern ones (Latin America, Africa) and this conclusion is inescapable.

I therefore believe that the conclusions to Gregory's research are as true for the UK as they are in the USA.

Most business people here would nowadays accept that advertising has a key role to play in building sales and long-term brand values. Even the most hawkish finance director who advocated cutting advertising budgets in a recession would raise eyebrows if he were to suggest cutting out advertising for ever.

There is also recent research from PIMS which demonstrates that maintenance of ad spend during the last two recessions has been associated with increased market share during the subsequent recoveries.

This research may seem therefore to do no more than confirm the common sense view (although this alone has value). However, crucially, this research establishes a link between ad spend and the achievement of a much more fundamental management objective – improvements in shareholder value. The conclusions need to be refined with additional research and it is to be hoped that a causal link can be established.

Nevertheless, even in this preliminary form this research is clearly relevant to all public company managers. But as an English accountant I find this work particularly exciting.

In the UK there is a strong trend towards the adoption of the technique of value-based management. This technique subordinates traditional accounting measures of performance to measures more closely linked to real value. Traditional accounting tools are therefore inadequate to provide the information needed to manage enterprises in this way.

The present accounting establishment is deeply sceptical about accounting for intangible assets, on the basis that if it can't be quantified it shouldn't be on the balance sheet. As such that part of the real value of a company which is represented by intangibles such as brands, trademarks or patents may simply not be represented in any form in a set of accounts prepared under present convention.

By providing a link between ad spending, brand values and thence to company share valuations, this research could be the first step to remedying this omission. If it is proved that money spent on advertising has as solid and demonstrable a value in investment terms as money spent on a piece of machinery, then the logic for capitalising brand investment on the balance sheet begins to be established. If this were to become accepted practice in accounting then management would be free from the pressure to cut the spend in a downturn and be better able to concentrate on long-term value creation.

The argument in brief: Chapter 3

The evidence from a special analysis of the PIMS database commissioned by the IPA, together with specific cases from the IPA's Databank of Awards cases, shows how advertising contributes to profitability over the long term.

- Advertising creates value by directly affecting perceived relative quality.
- Advertising achieves significant rewards for companies who sustain their advertising investment and thus maintain their relative quality perception over the long term.
- Even in difficult economic or trading conditions, continued advertising investment can be demonstrated to deliver returns.
- However, whatever their good intentions for thinking long term, many companies cut their ad spend when the going gets tough. But this strategy does not generally pay.
- Businesses that increased relative adspend during downturns in demand were significantly more profitable than those who cut or maintained it.
- Once recovery began, businesses that increased or maintained adspend during the downturn made the fastest profit improvement in the first 2 years of the recovery.
- Those who increased adspend during tough times increased their market share faster when recovery had started.

Chapter 3

Advertising and profitability: the long-term returns*

Marilyn Baxter

Introduction

It's almost ten years since the IPA first addressed the thorny issue of how to measure the long-term effects of advertising. The IPA's *Longer and Broader Effects of Advertising*[1] published in 1990 collected the then current thinking from the luminaries of the time, under the editorship of Chris Baker.

In his introduction, Chris pointed to the relative lack of work that had been done to date to evaluate the longer-term and more strategic effects of advertising on the building of valuable brands, on customer loyalty and on company profitability. Whereas his remarks condemning the short-termism of British business might easily have been written yesterday, it is pleasing to note that the intention behind this publication and the simultaneous introduction of the 'Longer and Broader' category in the Advertising Effectiveness Awards, has been very much realised. We *do* now have a number of general studies and specific cases that articulate and evaluate the longer-term effects of advertising.

Most interesting among the recent general studies is the work that has been done by benchmarking specialist PIMS Associates in collaboration with the IPA.[2] This partnership was formed to meet a growing demand from senior management for 'general proofs' of the value of advertising to set alongside the expanding Data Bank of individual Advertising Effectiveness Awards cases.

---

*This article first appeared in *Admap* in July 2000. It is reproduced here with kind permission from *Admap*.

In the business of producing persuasive evidence of the value of advertising, which is the remit of the Value of Advertising Committee, we continually come up against the paradox that the particular does not prove the general, and the general does not prove the particular. Indeed, some sceptics question the value of the Effectiveness Awards case histories on the grounds that they are *specific* cases and therefore the proofs are particular to a specific company and not of general value.

But they also question *general* analyses on the grounds that there is no such thing as the average company and the case does not prove what is true for any particular company. Our approach has therefore been to produce evidence both from general studies and specific cases, in order to provide some answers to the question: does advertising create long-term value for brands and for companies and, if so, how does it do it and can we measure the extent of that value?

To provide general evidence for the long-term value of advertising, the IPA has commissioned two special analyses from the PIMS database of over 3000 businesses worldwide. The first uses a sub-sample of 200 companies operating principally in branded consumer products in Europe. The results of this study were first published in September 1998 by Leslie Butterfield as an IPA AdValue paper, 'How advertising impacts on profitability'.[3] The second looks at a different sample of 183 companies in the UK who had experienced recessionary market conditions. The experiences of this particular group of companies were felt to be interesting because it is only when a company meets difficult trading conditions that its otherwise good intentions of holding faith with its belief in advertising are put to the test. Thus, difficult economic conditions are often the hurdle at which most long-term strategies fall, and so this analysis represents a kind of 'torture test' for the long-term value of advertising. In addition, and to provide specific case examples, a number of case studies from the IPA's Data Bank of some 650 Advertising Effectiveness Awards winners have been examined.

The relationship between advertising and profitability

The first PIMS study is valuable because it proves that there is a *causal* relationship (not just an associative one) between advertising spend and profitability, and because that relationship is not a simple or direct one, it also articulates the *way* in which advertising impacts on profitability.

The model found by the PIMS analysis is shown in Figure 3.1. The key findings are that:

■ Advertising impacts on profitability because it contributes to a key driver of profitability, namely relative customer value.

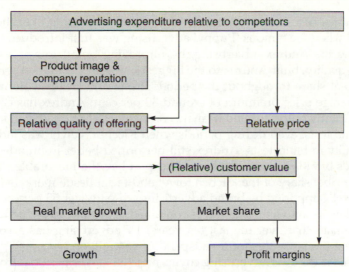

Figure 3.1 Links from advertising to profitability

- The key driver of relative customer value is perceived quality, and there is a direct correlation between advertising and (customer perceived) quality.
- Successful advertising is therefore that which builds product or service image and company reputation, both of which are key components of perceived quality.
- Successful advertising spends heavily relative to its share of the market: those brands or businesses that invest in advertising to produce share of voice over and above their share of market outperform their competition.
- It is not just 'any old advertising' that has this effect: spend alone is not enough. The style and content of advertising are also important. Advertising that focuses on product image, company reputation and/or other key attributes that drive customer perceptions of relative quality and hence value will be successful in business terms.

Causal relationships are rarely easy to demonstrate in discussions about advertising. This analysis, however, provides evidence that advertising works to create value for companies and provides a clear analysis of the way in which it works, as well as clear direction for advertisers as to *how* to spend their advertising money.

Long-term advertising examples

Some outstanding IPA Awards cases, especially those entered for the 'Longer and Broader' category, illustrate this model well.

The Andrex case from 1992 traces the effect of advertising over the 20 years from 1972 when the famous 'Puppy' advertising was first introduced. The case shows how the Andrex advertising, by improving brand image and relative perceived quality, built Andrex to the biggest brand in the market with around a 30 per cent share throughout the period, strong and steady volume growth, and an average price premium of around 30 per cent. Andrex has consistently and significantly outperformed its main competitor, Kleenex Velvet, in branded versus blind tests; even during periods when Kleenex Velvet was judged to be better quality in blind tests, Andrex still performed better in branded tests.

Andrex's brand strength has helped keep at bay the inexorable rise of own label: own-label share of the kitchen towel and facial tissue markets (neither of which is well supported by brand advertising) rose to over 55 per cent over the period, whereas in toilet tissue it was contained to around 40 per cent. The case study estimates that over the last ten years, TV advertising has accounted for £300 million of extra sales for an adspend of £54 million.[4]

The case for PG Tips advertising covers an even longer period – from 1956 to 1990. In response to the new advertising campaign featuring the PG Chimps, PG Tips grew rapidly from the fourth brand in 1956 to brand leadership in 1958, and *maintained* that leadership position throughout the next three decades with a consistently high and stable volume share, despite intense competitive pressure, own-label introductions, competitive promotions and a lower share of voice than competitors.[5]

Again, superior relative quality is shown to have been established through the advertising, not through the product quality: in blind tests consumers find it virtually impossible to discriminate between the brands but in branded tests PG Tips has enjoyed by far the highest preference in the market. This superior quality perception has translated through to price premium (PG Tips' price elasticity is only 0.4 compared with 1.4 for Tetley) and dominant brand share. The case proposes various methods of assessing the financial returns on the £100 million or so spent on advertising over the previous 20 years and produces estimates of up to £2 billion in extra sales as a result of the advertising.

Advertising in tough economic conditions

The clear message from PIMS about the causal relationship between advertising and profitability, together with the examples from the IPA Awards Data Bank, make a strong case for the value of advertising over the long term. This relationship appears to hold generally true regardless of economic conditions but, despite the evidence, many companies do not hold faith with advertising when market conditions deteriorate. Often advertising budgets are first to be cut when the going gets tough, so the IPA commissioned a second study from

PIMS, looking at how companies had behaved towards advertising during recessionary market conditions.

PIMS examined the profitability performance of some 183 companies operating in the UK who had experienced similar poor market conditions, not just in periods of general economic recession but of recessions in their own sectors or industries; these were grouped by whether they had maintained, cut, or increased their adspend relative to the size of their market.

The first conclusion that can be drawn from this analysis is that when the going gets tough, not many businesses get going. In looking at these businesses' strategies for dealing with recession, 110 chose to cut adspend, 53 chose to maintain it and only 20 chose to increase it.

But the results from these three groups of companies show that fortune favours the brave. Of course, most companies' profitability suffers in a downturn, but the PIMS analysis shows that those businesses that increased adspend were significantly more profitable during the downturn than those who cut or maintained it – nearly twice as profitable as the cutters, and nearly three times more profitable than the maintainers.

Once market recovery had started, businesses that maintained or increased adspend during the downturn made the fastest profit improvement: in the first two years of recovery, those that cut adspend during the tough times increased profits at only half the rate of those who increased adspend, and at only one-sixth of the rate of the maintainers.

And those who increased adspend during the tough times increased their market share faster when recovery had started than those who did not – nearly three times as fast as the advertising cutters.

Why advertising works in a downturn

So, continuing or increasing adspend during a downturn appears to have a positive effect on company profitability and market share. Why might that be? What is the mechanism by which advertising appears to work, even in a downturn in demand?

We selected a number of sectors of consumer expenditure and looked at what one might expect to happen to consumer purchasing behaviour and competitor behaviour in a slowdown (see Table 3.1).

The IPA Awards Data Bank is rich in examples of companies and brands in these sectors whose appreciation of the long-term value of advertising enabled them to resist recessionary pressures. Two cases in particular stand out – one in premium fmcg, Nestlé's Gold Blend, the other durables – BMW cars.

The Nescafé Gold Blend case from 1996 tracks the performance of the well-known 'romance' campaign over a ten-year period. During this period, the advertising budget remained largely unchanged at around £5 million per

Table 3.1 Dealing with recession: roles for advertising

	What do we expect to happen in a slowdown?	What can advertising do to counteract these effects
Durables	Put off investment in new products. Hold onto existing products for longer. Trade down to cheaper alternatives	Stimulate sales by providing a reason to buy. Add perceived value to trade off against higher price
Fmcg	Trade down to cheaper/less good quality substitutes. Don't risk buying new products	Add perceived value to trade off against higher price. Inform persuasively about new products
Discretionary purchases	Cut down on discretionary items. Trade down to cheaper alternatives	Stimulates sales by providing a reason to buy. Add perceived value to trade off against higher price
Competitors cut marketing budgets	Depresses demand by removing stimulus to buy	Stimulate sales by providing a reason to buy

annum. The case shows how the advertising projected an upmarket, sophisticated image that communicated quality. This strong quality reputation resulted in Gold Blend becoming brand leader with a 40 per cent share, which enabled it to maintain its price premium and to resist the onslaught of competitive activity, especially from heavily price-promoted own-label introductions. This success continued during the recession of the early 1990s, during a period when it would be expected that many buyers would trade down to cheaper alternatives.

The case shows how, even during recession, Gold Blend's sales continued to grow, its price premium relative to Nescafé remained unchanged, and there was no evidence of trading down. A sustained advertising investment of some £5 million per annum has resulted in extra long-term sales of £50 million per annum due to the recruitment and retention of new and loyal buyers.

The car sector has historically been very hard hit by the economic cycle, but a number of cases from the IPA Data Bank show how good advertising has helped some brands resist or even counteract recessionary pressures. The most outstanding of these is, arguably, BMW. A core brand value of BMW is quality (expressed through an image of performance, advanced technology and exclusivity). These values have been consistently and clearly communicated through a UK-only advertising campaign for some 20 years now.

The 1994 IPA case tracks the first 15 years of the campaign, and shows how the superior quality imagery and reputation of BMW enabled the marque to treble sales, maintain prices (price rose faster than the market average, even during the last recession), and retain its exclusivity. The case estimates, by comparing UK sales performance with other European countries that did not have this advertising, that the extra strength of the brand, created largely by the advertising, was worth around £3 billion in extra sales over the 15 years, for a total adspend of £91 million.

All the examples quoted above support the PIMS model that relative perceived quality is a key driver of market share and thus profitability, although they are all campaigns that achieved their results without having to outspend the competition. Indeed, in some of the examples, most notably PG Tips and BMW, their share of voice was relatively low (BMW's was at the same level as Proton's in 1994). A possible conclusion is that the creative content – the quality of the advertising itself also matters: the better the advertising that focuses on product quality, the more cost-effective it is.

Conclusion

The combination of the general data of aggregated business performance provided by PIMS and the cases from the IPA of specific brands and specific advertising campaigns adds up to a persuasive case for the long-term value of advertising to brands and businesses. Clearly though, this does not provide us with a simple formula – spend money on advertising and you are certain of success. Marketers and advertising agencies must recognise where advertising fits in their own mix, the brand's own strategic market position, objectives for growth and profitability, and external market factors, in order to understand how to make advertising work for them over the long term.

References

1. Baker, C. (ed.), *The Longer and Broader Effects of Advertising*, IPA, 1990.
2. See also Hillier, T., 'Are you profiting from marketing?' *Admap*, January 1999.
3. Butterfield, L., 'How advertising impacts on profitability', *ADVALUE*, Issue One, IPA, September 1998.
4. Feldwick, P., *Advertising Works 6*, NTC Publications Ltd, 1991.
5. Barwise, P. (ed.), *Advertising in a Recession*, NTC Publications Ltd, July 1999.

The argument in brief: Chapter 4

- Shareholder value is a function of the future cash flows a business is likely to generate.
- 'Market-based assets', especially the relationships the firm has through its brands with its customers, can significantly affect those cash flows.
- Advertising is a powerful 'lever' of those market-based assets.
- Three short-term effects can be identified:
    - accelerating the speed of cash flows
    - enhancing the value of cash flows
    - reducing the volatility of cash flows.
- Beyond these, advertising can also affect long-term cash flows, which is reflected in their residual value in the present day.
- All the above impact on brand value and hence shareholder value today.

Chapter 4

How advertising affects shareholder value

Leslie Butterfield

Introduction

The IPA is at the forefront of trying to promote a greater understanding of the financial value attributable to brands as a key measure of advertising effectiveness. For many years the focus in the advertising industry has been on the bottom half of the hierarchy shown in Figure 4.1. The IPA's Effectiveness Awards scheme has concentrated, historically, on short-term advertising effects

Figure 4.1 A hierarchy of advertising effect

on sales and share and not enough on the harder-to-quantify effects on brand or even company value.

The IPA has already sought to broaden the criteria by which the Advertising Effectiveness Awards are judged, to take account of this expanded definition of advertising's role. Its mission now is to try to elevate the debate up the hierarchy shown here by demonstrating that *brand valuation* can be a key measure of advertising effectiveness and that therefore it brings a whole new slant to marketing and advertising budget decisions. Even if only used as an internal tool, brand valuation gets all disciplines within a branded business to focus on the asset value of their brands, which in turn leads to those other disciplines viewing advertising expenditures as investments rather than just costs.

Advertising, market-based assets and cash flow

It is increasingly expected that agencies should take responsibility for the effectiveness of their work for a client; effectiveness in all senses, including financial accountability. The ultimate contribution an agency can make is enhancing the shareholder value of its clients' business.

While brand valuation is a useful and important method for measuring the contribution of brands to the total value of a business, it doesn't of itself explain *how* advertising contributes to brand value (and hence shareholder value).

A lot of the interest in the whole issue of advertising and shareholder value is coming out of the USA. But among the various papers on the subject, one stands out above the rest: 'Market based assets and shareholder value' by Srivastava, Shervani and Fahey, delivered at the US Marketing Science Institute, in 1998.

The paper talks about a 'quiet revolution' in the way that marketing activities are being viewed by some marketing professionals, by CEOs and by enlightened finance directors. In a nutshell, what the paper argues is that marketers will increasingly be called upon to view their ultimate purpose as contributing to the enhancement of financial returns. This in turn will mean that customers (and indeed distribution channels) will be viewed as 'market-based assets' that need to be captured, cultivated and leveraged. In tandem, marketers will need to move beyond traditional measures such as sales, share and margin to measures based on maximising the net present value of future cash flows... and hence shareholder value.

Two things are worth clarifying at this point. Firstly, by the 'net present value of future cash flows', we mean the value *today* of the income streams likely to accrue to the company, over, say, a five-year period. That income is discounted at a rate which takes account of the degree of uncertainty that attaches to it.

Secondly, of the 'market-based assets' that the authors refer to, the most significant for us are what they call 'relational assets' – which are principally the relationships between a firm and its consumers. To quote: 'Brand equity reflects the bonds between a firm and its customer and may be the result of extensive advertising and superior product functionality.'

So how do market-based assets specifically affect the shareholder value of the business? At its simplest, the market value of a firm is the net present value of all future cash flows expected to accrue to the firm. The importance of this perspective is underlined by the fact that a large proportion of the value of firms is based on perceived growth potential and associated risks. That value is based on *expectations* of future performance.

Because shareholder value is largely composed of the present value of cash flows during a defined period, the value of any strategy is inherently driven by:

1 Accelerating the *speed* with which cash flows are generated (earlier cash flows are preferred because risk and time adjustments reduce the value of later cash flows).
2 An increase in the *level* of cash flows generated through its various components (e.g. higher revenues and lower costs, working capital, and fixed investments).
3 A reduction in *risk* associated with future cash flows (e.g. via reduction in both volatility and vulnerability of future cash flows), hence, indirectly, the firm's cost of capital.

Now, if we take each of these three shareholder value drivers, let's examine how marketing and advertising activity can affect and enhance each one in turn:

1 *Accelerating cash flows*: The authors cite evidence from numerous published studies that demonstrate that leveraging market-based assets (for example, through advertising) can accelerate cash flows by increasing the responsiveness of the marketplace to marketing activity, e.g. speeding up trial, adoption and referral rates for new or next generation products or brand extensions from the same company (see Figure 4.2).
2 *Increasing or enhancing cash flows:* The authors here cite examples of enhanced cash flows as a result of:
   (a) established brands being able to command a price premium
   (b) higher customer retention and therefore lower customer 'recruitment' costs
   (c) greater responsiveness of loyal customers to advertising and promotions (therefore lower marginal costs of sales and marketing)
   (d) greater uptake of brand extensions (see Figure 4.3).
3 *Influencing the volatility of cash flows*: Volatility (and vulnerability) of cash flows is reduced when customer satisfaction, loyalty and retention are increased. Importantly the net present value of a less volatile cash flow is greater than that of a more erratic one – again contributing directly to shareholder value (see Figure 4.4).

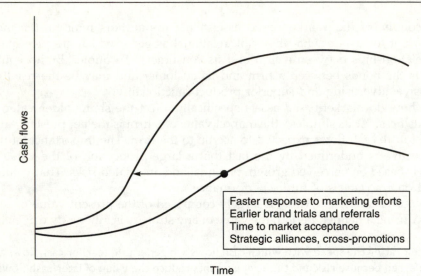

Faster response to marketing efforts
Earlier brand trials and referrals
Time to market acceptance
Strategic alliances, cross-promotions

Figure 4.2 Accelerating cash flows

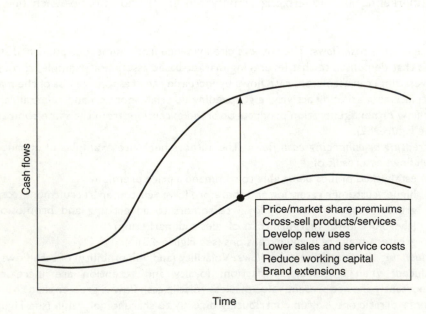

Price/market share premiums
Cross-sell products/services
Develop new uses
Lower sales and service costs
Reduce working capital
Brand extensions

Figure 4.3 Enhancing cash flows

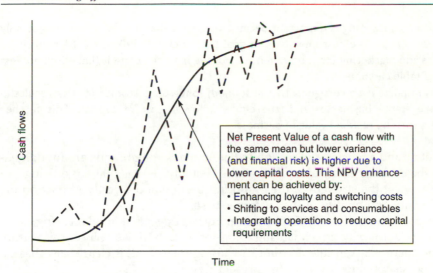

Figure 4.4 Reducing the volatility of cash flows

The bottom line (literally) is that advertising affects the quality of a brand's relationship with its customers, which in turn can be demonstrated to affect cash flow, which directly impacts on shareholder value.

Advertising and the residual value of cash flows

Residual value is the present value of a business attributed to cash flows that are likely to accrue *beyond* the normal forecasting horizon (usually 5 years). This value is often shown as an 'annuity' added to the brand value calculation for the 5-year period. Again though, as with the 5-year horizon, residual value reflects expectations of future cash flows – and these, for a brand with a life expectancy that may run to decades, will clearly be significant.

The resulting 'annuity' will therefore account for a significant proportion of the *current* net present value of the business – and hence current shareholder value.

To quote again from the Srivastava paper:

Some of the same factors that contribute to enhancing cash flows, and reducing volatility and vulnerability, also lead to higher residual values. For instance, the larger the customer base, and the higher the quality of the customer base (as measured by usage volume, willingness to pay a price premium, lower sales and service costs, etc), the higher the loyalty (and, therefore, the lower the risk or vulnerability), thus the higher the residual value.

This understanding is important because to create shareholder value we not only have to grow the customer base (a goal that is closely linked to the traditional sales and marketing focus on revenue), but we have to refine it (i.e. eliminate less profitable customers).

It is important to recognise that sustained, long-run customer loyalty results in more stable businesses and, therefore, a lower cost of capital. This further enhances the residual value of business.

Marketers and agencies will see immediately that strong brands are fundamental to the chain of events described above. Equally clear is that advertising can directly affect the strength of the brand in question and directly impact on the size, loyalty and quality of the customer base.

Just as with short-term effects, this analysis suggests that advertising has a crucial role to play in enhancing long-term cash flows. Since this future enhancement is taken into account in valuing the brand, it clearly also has an effect on shareholder value in the present day.

Advertising, price promotion and cash flows

In a later paper, delivered at the MAX conference in New York, Srivastava develops the argument further, comparing the differential effects on cash flows of advertising and price promotions.

While acknowledging the short-term impact of the latter, he points out that price promotions can, however, erode long-term cash flows, by producing a vicious circle (see Figure 4.5).

'The way to break the cycle,' says Srivastava 'is to build brands, which involves differentiation, and thus advertising.' Brands not only maintain higher price premiums, they also build loyalty – which is valuable both in smoothing cash flows and in reducing defection rates. With customer acquisition costs running at up to five times retention costs, lower defection rates translate directly into higher net present values and lower cost of capital.

Conclusion

Brand valuation points the way forward in terms of quantifying the contribution of advertising to company value. But it is through the analysis and understanding of advertising's effect on cash-flows that we can best understand *how* advertising has this effect.

Recent evidence from the USA highlights the business value of 'market-based assets'. Advertising can directly leverage those assets, affecting short- and long-term cash flows, and hence the ultimate value of the firm.

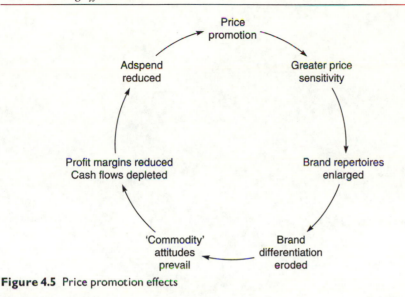

Figure 4.5 Price promotion effects

Market-based assets, especially 'relational assets' such as brands and relationships with customers and distribution channels, don't yet appear on many balance sheets. But they can be valued, they can be bought and sold and they can be leveraged and utilised in just the same way as physical assets.

What's more, they are assets that more often appreciate than depreciate, unlike many tangibles!

Advertising has a key role to play in stimulating those assets, growing their worth and hence creating shareholder value.

PART B

Business Performance Effects

The argument in brief: Chapter 5

Advertising is capable of three types of effect: *short-term* (effect on sales within a week of exposure); *medium-term* (effect of sales over the course of a year); and *long-term* (effect on a brand beyond a year and into the future). It is extremely important for advertisers to evaluate the marketplace performance of their campaigns and invest only in the productive ones. The longer the period over which we measure the results of campaigns, the more difficult the measurement becomes. However, the advertising industry is developing very quickly its measurement skills, and the situation in future years will probably be well in advance of what it is today.

Chapter 5

How advertising drives sales and profit

John Philip Jones

Introduction

Advertising is an activity of the first importance to most marketing companies, for two good reasons. The first and obvious one is that advertising is capable of contributing to a major degree to the short-term sales and the long-term health of manufacturers' brands.

The second reason is more subtle and is particularly relevant to advertisers who are contemplating increasing their investments. The amount of money that advertisers spend on their campaigns is often not too different from the profit their brands earn, *and both sums are residuals*. For instance, the number two advertiser in the United States, Procter & Gamble (P&G), in 1998 spent $2.6 billion on advertising in measured and unmeasured media, and the firm earned $2.7 billion in profit. An increase in P&G's advertising budget of 10 per cent would have cut into profit by almost the same percentage. It is obvious therefore that any extra expenditure on advertising must be required to boost sales and profit to a healthy degree if it is not to be a drag on the business, i.e. producing a cost greater than the return.

One of the serious problems with advertising is that it is difficult to measure the sales and profit that it generates. Most business people, marketers and agencies alike, have learned from their general experience that advertising is capable of improving the position of many brands, and that it would indeed be difficult to imagine PG Tips, Kellogg's Corn Flakes, Persil, American Express, Ford and Orange, and many other brands, being where they are today without successful advertising both past and present. But quantifying precisely what advertising has contributed to these and other important brands is a different question altogether.

It is not difficult to track on a continuous basis people's awareness of brands and the rational and non-rational attributes they associate with them: psychological measures rather than behavioural ones. However, psychological measures are both too insensitive and too 'soft' (i.e. fuzzy and indirect) to provide a firm basis for us to evaluate and eventually justify the financial cost of advertising. For this task we need 'hard' measures related to consumer purchasing.

Nevertheless, there are some things about measurement that we know for certain and other things we know impressionistically. The state of our knowledge is improving quite rapidly, and the British advertising community should be constantly reminded of the contribution to our understanding that has been made during the past two decades by the IPA's formidable battery of *Advertising Effectiveness* cases. There is nothing to be compared with them in range and quality in any other country around the world.

One thing we know quite positively is that advertising is capable of three orders of effect. This does not mean that these three effects are always achieved.

■ *Short-term*: the influence of advertising on sales of a brand within seven days of its exposure.
■ *Medium-term*: the accumulation of short-term effects across the course of a year.
■ *Long-term*: a progressive series of effects that can operate over a period of years and which are represented by an enrichment of the brand itself and a strengthening of the user's buying behaviour.

Our ability to measure these three effects differs one from another; the long-term effect is by far the most elusive one to capture. But again we have good evidence for one conclusion. A short-term effect is a precondition for a medium-term one and a medium-term effect is a precondition for a long-term one. This seems to be common sense, but we must remember that for many years large numbers of advertisers and advertising agencies believed the myth that advertising can drip away to no apparent effect and then eventually produce an explosion. This 'time bomb' hypothesis was responsible for spectacular waste resulting from the continued exposure of ineffective advertising – an outcome supported by nothing except blind optimism.

Short-term effect

The short-term effect of advertising has been familiar to practitioners of direct response for the whole period – a century at least – during which this type of advertising has been successfully practised. But a short-term effect is not exclusive to advertising that is explicitly planned to work directly.

An expensive technique called Pure Single-Source research makes it possible to measure advertising's short-term influence on the sales of brands of fast-moving consumer goods (fmcg). This is a method of comparing the buying of a brand in households which have received advertising for it during the previous seven days with buying in households which have not received such advertising. The typical range of such effects is shown in Table 5.1.

In each of the three countries covered, a substantial sample of brands have been measured, and their campaigns have been ranked from the most to the least effective, and divided into 10 per cent groups (deciles). The average short-term sales effect is indexed on 100 (equivalent to no effect). Thus, in the top decile in the United Kingdom, the average brand achieved a short-term sales improvement of 84 per cent; in the bottom decile, the average brand lost 27 per cent of sales. The reductions in the bottom 30 per cent of campaigns (a consistent picture for the United States, the United Kingdom and Germany) are caused by the brands using advertising that is not strong enough to protect them from the more powerful advertising for competitors; and consumers therefore choose the alternatives.

Note that in all these countries about half of all advertising has a pronounced short-term effect. The informed guess made a century ago by William Hesketh Lever and John Wanamaker that 50 per cent of their advertising was effective was substantially correct. But we have made an important advance in our

Table 5.1 Range of short-term effects (STAS) in three countries

Decile	United States	United Kingdom	Germany
Top	236	184	154
Ninth	164	129	127
Eighth	139	119	116
Seventh	121	114	108
Sixth	116	110	106
Fifth	108	107	101
Fourth	103	102	100
Third	97	98	98
Second	89	93	92
Bottom	73	73	83

knowledge. While these two ancient experts were unable to identify the successful 50 per cent, this is now totally within our capacity.

Pure Single-Source research shows conclusively that a substantial sales effect is felt in purchases of households that have been exposed to a single advertisement. This suggests strongly that it is the creative quality of the campaign that drives the short-term effect, and not the financial factors of budget and media.

Medium-term effect

The end of a year is normally stock-taking time for a brand. This process includes a review of the advertising, which is normally carried out in a rough-and-ready fashion: if sales are ahead, green light; if they are stagnant or declining, red light.

What year-end sales represent, as far as the consumer advertising is concerned, is the net accumulation of short-term effects. By 'net', I mean the repeated short-term effects of our brand's campaigns, minus the repeated short-term effects of other brands' campaigns. The latter generally work most strongly when our brand is off the air: when it is vulnerable.

The medium-term effect of a brand's advertising is the result of the creative quality of the campaign, *plus the budget and the media strategy*, in particular the degree to which the budget and media strategy reduce the number of weeks the brand is not advertised.

Since the medium-term effect of advertising is influenced by the countervailing influence of competitors' advertising, the effect is invariably less than the short-term effect. A brand with a successful campaign that boosts sales in the short term by 50 per cent would be lucky to end the year 10 per cent ahead. And we must be careful to isolate how much of this 10 per cent is due to advertising and how much to other sales stimuli.

The most commonly used device to make such an estimate is regression analysis, which can make two calculations that have operational importance.

1 It can deconstruct a brand's sales during a year (or any other period) and break out the elements contributing to those sales. Advertising rarely contributes more than 10 per cent; sales promotions rarely more than another 10 per cent. The residual 80 per cent (plus) is described at the brand's 'base' or 'equity' volume – the quantity of sales that would have been made without any advertising or sales promotions at all.

2 It can calculate an advertising elasticity, which measures the effect on sales of increments (up or down) in a brand's expenditure on advertising. The actual figure is calculated as the percentage change in a brand's sales that results from a 1 per cent change in advertising expenditure. From a large sample of brands, there is usually

an approximate 5:1 relationship e.g. a 5 per cent boost in advertising can on average be expected to increase sales by 1 per cent.

Long-term effects

As mentioned, the long-term effects (in the plural) are the most difficult ones to measure. This is because they are embedded in the brand itself, and extracting the influence attributable to advertising alone is exceptionally difficult. A helpful way to look at this problem is to ask how much of the brand's 'base' or 'equity' sales volume actually represents the cumulative result of previous advertising.

It is not difficult to find measures to compare a strong brand with a weak one. Here are six (and they may not be an exclusive list). But in every case, we must bear in mind the problem of isolating advertising's specific contribution.

1 A strong brand will generally (although not invariably) have a larger share of market than a weak brand.
2 A strong brand will generally command a higher consumer price than a weak one; sales promotions are a less important business driver for a strong brand.
3 A strong brand will tend to have above-average purchase frequency, and a weak brand will have below-average. This is a technical measure of consumer loyalty.
4 Because of the endemic power of a strong brand (expressed by the above-average 'base' or 'equity' sales level), consumers respond to its advertising more positively than they do to the advertising of a weak brand. A strong brand can advertise relatively less than a weak brand and still achieve the same effect. I have coined the term Advertising-Intensiveness Bonus (AIB) to describe this effect.
5 The advertising elasticity of a strong brand is likely to be higher than for a weak one. This means that advertising works hard if it is building on the endemic strength of the brand.
6 There is also a factor concerning the price elasticity of demand: the response of sales to a measured increase or decrease in consumer price. Price elasticity is a precise expression of how easily consumers will substitute another brand if the price of our brand is increased. The price elasticity of a strong brand is likely to be less than that of a weak brand, because consumers will be *less* willing to substitute other brands if the strong brand's price goes up.

At the moment we cannot robustly isolate the influence of advertising on most of these factors. An exception is point 4, for which a measure has already been developed. With regard to the other measures, provisional work on them led to a book, *The Ultimate Secrets of Advertising*, published in 2002.

Conclusion: Bridging the gap in our knowledge

If and when we manage to measure accurately the total contribution of advertising to the value of a brand's sales, the advertiser will inevitably wish to compare (a) this contribution to (b) the actual cost of the advertising.

Prima facie, most examples that have been produced to date do not succeed in demonstrating that (a) is larger than (b). Does this represent an indictment of advertising as a commercial enterprise? This is not necessarily the case, for two reasons.

First, a brand in any year produces a volume of sales not dissimilar from the volume of the year before and also that of the preceding year. The cost structure of a brand is based on a broadly defined sales level: a level at which scale economies (in raw material purchasing, in manufacturing and in marketing) come strongly into play. These economies mean that the unit cost is generally a good deal less than at a smaller volume of sales. It can therefore be trenchantly argued that previous and current advertising, *by merely maintaining a high sales volume*, contributes to the profitability of a brand by its ability to hold manufacturers' costs to a low level.

The second point is that the long-term effect of advertising – as and when we are able to measure it – can legitimately be added to the medium-term effect (which we commonly measure anyway).

A gap, however, still exists between the medium-term effect we *can* quantify and the additional long-term effect which exists but which at the moment we cannot evaluate accurately. But I am optimistic about the tools that are being developed to help us build a bridge over this gap.

The argument in brief: Chapter 6

The IPA Advertising Effectiveness Data Bank demonstrates significant quantifiable benefits of advertising in the complex arena of face-to-face financial services selling, for which the maxim has traditionally been that products are sold, not bought. The Data Bank findings argue that this maxim is untrue, by identifying and quantifying the following manifold effects of financial services advertising:

- Increasing brand consideration
- Improving direct response rates
- Enhancing the success rate in securing sales appointments and in prospects keeping their sales appointments
- Improving overall conversion rates of prospects across a lengthy sales process
- Encouraging referrals
- Reducing lapsing
- Building repeat purchase – either multiple sales or reinvestment on maturity
- Motivating and raising the productivity of the sales force

It is important to examine these effects individually when constructing a business case for advertising, because each effect may carry its own cost implication for the business as well as a benefit. Overall the IPA Data Bank reports some very healthy returns on investment in the financial services category that should encourage wavering advertisers. The data exists within the 700 Data Bank case studies to conduct similar predictive modelling in most categories.

Chapter 6

How advertising impacts the sales process

Peter Field

Introduction

Advertising agencies are asked ever more often to help their marketing clients justify proposed advertising budgets to general management. This is difficult enough to answer in the relatively straightforward case of a fast-moving consumer good. But what about where there is a complex sales chain involving sales agents, word-of-mouth referrals, lengthy repeat purchase cycles and so on? Sceptical general management may have trouble acknowledging a worthwhile effect directly on consumers, let alone the numerous manifold effects that are essential to consider in a complex sales process. In particular, how do you justify advertising investment in the situation where conventional wisdom suggests that products are *'sold, not bought'*? Surely it is all down to the skill and persistence of the salespeople? It is one thing to say that it 'oils the wheels' of the sales process and another to prove that it can happen or to quantify the extent of the benefit.

This chapter reports an attempt to use the IPA Data Bank to justify advertising investment for a financial services company to its board. In so doing, it looks at a number of ways in which advertising would affect the company's sales performance, with supporting evidence. Where this justification differs from others is that for some measures it is able to use the Data Bank *quantitatively*, examining average effects over many case studies. In so doing it attempts to escape the usual accusations of an individual case being a special case, and thus provides a generalised justification. More importantly, it enables more rigorous forecasting of the realistic scale of the effects. The analysis is necessarily approximate: it would be misleading to attempt to define an average too precisely as the circumstances of any campaign or company are never average. The output is an expected set of effects, each of which is then valued through to its impact on the bottom line of the company. The analysis therefore can be used at two levels: simply to demonstrate that advertising can have manifold benefits for a complex sales process or more subtly to forecast the sales response and organisational demands resulting from advertising.

There are, I know, many people in advertising who will feel very nervous at the prospect of predicting possible outcomes of advertising. Nobody wants to create a rod for his or her own back. But the alternative may be to allow someone from the client's finance department to set wholly unrealistic expectations of marketing that the agency has no influence over. Or more likely, that the budget is cut in favour of more predictable investments. The kind of analysis reported here is a better alternative.

Of the 60 or so financial services papers in the Data Bank, some 25 were selected for this analysis, because they examined relevant kinds of effects in relevant situations. It would be possible to repeat this analysis in other markets, though some of the observations made here should be broadly applicable.

The sales model

The sales model to which this analysis was applied is shown in Figure 6.1. It is a perfectly standard financial services sales model, where a direct sales force is involved as well as a direct marketing effort. Without advertising, customers enter the sales chain either when contacted by a salesperson or when they respond to DM. The law requires two sales visits, and there are opportunities for multiple product sales as well as reinvestment sales when a product matures. There is the ever-present danger with long-term products of lapsing during the term, as well as the opportunity to gain referrals from satisfied customers. It is a long and complex sales process, when viewed from this lifetime value perspective. The challenge lies not in developing the model (which is an essential step in the process), but in getting the data that defines the current working of the business: how many sales appointments are made, how many are kept, how many are successful, etc. Each step affects the payback calculations: e.g. doubling the number of appointments will mean hiring new salespeople, whereas doubling the success rate will not.

The IPA Data Bank demonstrates that there are eight areas of this sales model that brand advertising benefits:

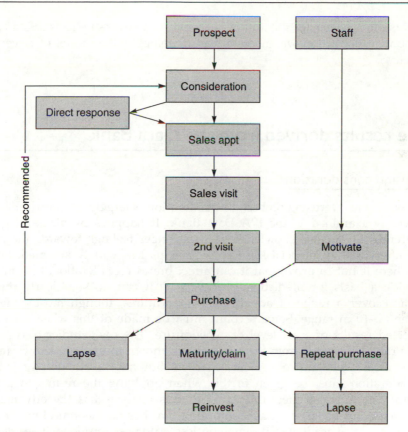

Figure 6.1 Simplified sales model of a direct sale financial services company

- Consideration
- Direct response rates
- Appointment making and keeping rates
- Purchasing (conversion from consideration to purchase)
- Referral (recommendation)
- Lapse/defection rates
- Repeat purchase/reinvestment on maturity
- Sales force motivation and productivity

Not all are affected equally and the bottom-line effect of a 10 per cent improvement in one area will not be the same as in another area. So each must be considered in isolation.

The financial services papers of the IPA Data Bank were searched for cases that observed these effects. In practice, of course, life was not that simple, because many of the cases don't break effects down into these neat categories (it was often neater for the authors to look at the overall effects). So a certain amount of deduction was necessary in developing the model of advertising effect.

The results derived from the Data Bank

1. Brand consideration

The effect of advertising on brand consideration is largely uncontroversial and is widely examined in the IPA Data Bank. It happens by virtue of greater awareness of, greater knowledge of, or stronger feelings towards the brand. The effect within financial services is perhaps less widely accepted, but the task here is not to prove that it can affect brand consideration, but rather to provide a basis for predicting *by how much* it can do so. Clearly the case studies cover a range of advertising expenditures, though mostly they fall in the £2–10 m range. Some account must be made of this when calculating expected results of a set level of expenditure. The case studies also cover a wide range of brands from the relatively unknown to the well known (and in some cases well known in some markets but not in others). Again some consideration must be given to this when applying the results to a given brand. The average effect calculated in this analysis has the advantage of simplicity, but makes a crude assumption that has no theoretical justification. However, since academics disagree on less crude assumptions, it seems legitimate. A linear average of effects is calculated (where there is plenty of data) and a linear average of the expenditures (national equivalent) taken. Clearly it is not the case that if you spend twice as much you will necessarily get twice the return. You may get less in some circumstances and more in others, but it is not unreasonable for a simple model to make the linear assumption. Table 6.1 demonstrates the range of expenditures and the associated effects on brand consideration. (NB: consideration levels in a number of market segments are reported for some brands.)

2. Direct response rates

The effect of brand advertising on direct response rates to direct mail and off-the-page advertising has been widely explored in the Data Bank. The effect is over and above the increased consideration of the brand – consumers are more likely to notice and study the DM piece and be persuaded to respond to it. The financial services examples are shown in Table 6.2.

Table 6.1 Shifts in brand consideration and associated advertising spend

Case	Spend (£m)	Consideration shift % to %
Frizzell	6	22–45
		17–38
C&G	8	7–11
Co-op	1.8	22–33
TSB	3.2	13–22
A&L	22	12–24
		7–15
Direct Line	1.3	10–20
Scot Am	3	3–7
Swinton	2	25–36
TSB	1.7	25–36
		30–47
		34–47
		36–44
		7–14
		10–18
Average	**5.4**	**17–27 (+60%)**

Table 6.2 Shifts in direct response rates and associated brand advertising spend

Case	Spend (£m)	Direct response rate (±%)
Frizzell	6	+78%
Direct Line	1.3	+40%
Mortgage Corp	1.2	+100%

3. Face-to-face meetings

The impact of advertising on success rates in securing sales appointments is a less well documented area in the Data Bank. However, there was one paper that examined this and provides at least some basis for justification (Table 6.3).

Given the level of consumer suspicion and fear surrounding financial services selling, advertising plays a powerful role in reassuring the customer that the company has a good reputation and one that it would not jeopardise. To some extent this is true of all face-to-face selling.

Table 6.3 Shifts in
sales appointment
volumes and associated
brand advertising spend

Case	Spend (£m)	Sales (±%)
A&L	3	+100%

Since this data measures the increase in appointments amongst cold pro-spects, it includes the effect on brand consideration, which must then be fac-tored out when building the effects model.

4. Purchasing

The overall effect of brand advertising on increased purchasing among pro-spects is widely documented and many financial services cases were available for analysis (Table 6.4).

There are many ways in which advertising helps move a brand from con-sideration to purchase in a complex sales process. In particular, with highly

Table 6.4 Shifts in purchasing among prospects and associated advertising expenditure

Case	Spend (£m)	Purchasing (±%)
C&G	8	+104%
Co-op	1.8	+49%
Halifax	1.5	+30%
Visa		+9%
TSB	3.2	+82%
A&L	22	+120%
	3	+30%
	2.6	+10%
Barclaycard	8	+5%
Swinton	2	+8%
TSB	1.7	+52%
	3.2	+40%
Allied Dunbar	10.4	+2%
Average	**5.4**	**41%**

regulated sales that may take weeks to close, the emotional reassurance that advertising builds can be helpful in keeping the customer 'on the rails'.

Once again this data measures the increase in purchasing amongst the universe of cold prospects and by a multitude of purchasing methods, so in our model it covers a number of steps (Figure 6.2) that must be factored out when building the final effects model. Clearly there are some rough and ready assumptions being made here in comparing overall effects for very different kinds of financial service organisations, but there is a limit, even with a database the size of the IPA's, to how precisely you can choose your reference points.

5. Referrals

Recommendation or referral rates have been observed to rise by a number of case studies but no accurate quantification appears to have been made. So for the purposes of this model, it is assumed that the rate of recommendation rises by the same proportion as the propensity to meet a salesperson. This is not as arbitrary as it may seem; each is a measure of the comfort of committing to the first meeting. Advertising may achieve this in two ways. It may partly strengthen the customer's feelings towards the company and hence perceptions of how well the company has served him or her. And by increasing the 'fame' of the company it may raise the customer's confidence in asking a friend to receive them.

6. Lapsing

The effect of advertising upon 'lapse' rates has been examined by a couple of financial services papers (Table 6.5). Again we are looking at somewhat different sectors here, but they do nevertheless provide a useful quantified measure of the potential growth of customer loyalty.

The means by which advertising supports loyalty is, as with referrals, by strengthening customer feelings towards the company. Mistakes or upsets are more likely to be forgiven and successes more likely to be applauded. This is

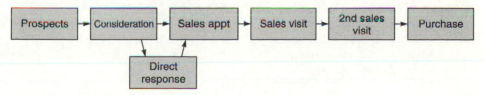

Figure 6.2 Sales steps from prospect to first purchase

Table 6.5 Reduction of lapse/defection
rates and associated adspend

Case	Spend (£m)	Lapse Rate (±%)
Co-op	1.8	−30%
Barclaycard	40	−10%

especially important with long-term products where there may be many temptations to drift away.

7. Repeat purchase

Repeat purchase is another area where increases are reported for financial services, but not quantified, so the assumption is made here that repeat purchase experiences the same improvement that is observed for lapsing. This seems a reasonable assumption since they are essentially opposite sides of the same coin: commitment to the brand.

This is an important business area for companies such as this, who review their customers from time to time and may see an opportunity to sell to them again.

8. Sales force motivation

Since this analysis was conducted, the effect of advertising on sales force productivity in other sectors has been verified by a number of the 1998 papers (e.g. Christian Aid and Littlewoods). For this analysis there is only one financial services paper to base a forecast on (Table 6.6). This is a complex area for forecasting. Increased productivity is largely a result of the number of appointments made for the sales force and the ease of converting a prospect: these are consequent of improved consumer consideration, already factored in to our

Table 6.6 Increase in staff productivity
and associated adspend

Case	Spend (£m)	Sales productivity (±%)
TSB	1.7	+22%

model. In particular for the company in question, the salespeople were already highly successful when they met prospects face-to-face, so there is little value to be gained here from advertising. What is being evaluated here is the multiplier effect of the additional energy, commitment and confidence of the sales force that results from them feeling supported by advertising. This can manifest itself in a number of ways that improve business results: e.g. shorter appointments thanks to quicker closing, more frequent multiple sales per appointment as well as greater persistence with tricky customers.

This chapter has demonstrated that the IPA Data Bank is able to validate and to some extent quantify the manifold effects of advertising in a complex sales chain. However, applying these effects together without the benefit of regression analysis, calls for some educated guesswork. The effects model below (Figure 6.3) is a reasonable, but approximate attempt to fit the individual effects to the overall model for an 'average' expenditure of £5–7 m, assuming the advertising is as fully effective as IPA papers show that it can be. Since the

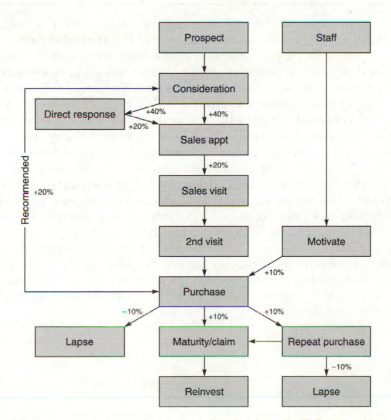

Figure 6.3 Approximate expected impacts on the sales chain of a £5–7 million advertising spend

IPA financial services papers cover just about every sector of the market, it is not unreasonable to target effectiveness on this scale for this expenditure level.

One point to note is that no improvement to the sale closing rate is being forecast (because of the high level of success already experienced by this particular sales force). Clearly this will not always be the case, but there is little evidence in the Data Bank, beyond the anecdotal (e.g. Scottish Amicable) of measured effects on face-to-face sales effectiveness in financial services, apart from the motivational productivity effect already described. This is not altogether surprising given the regulatory constraints on salesmanship – advertising's principal effect is in securing more face-to-face meetings for the sales force, rather than in making the meetings more successful.

Financial evaluation and conclusion

The purpose of such a detailed piecewise analysis is to enable a realistic payback calculation to be made that takes account of the associated costs of each advertising effect. In the particular case of the company concerned with this model, the strong annual premium growth forecast was significantly mitigated by a 23 per cent increase in sales force workload, that could only be met by hiring. Happily there remained an acceptable ROI in year 1, as well as the ongoing benefits of securing more long-term customers and losing fewer of them each year. This should not be considered an unusual or 'lucky' case; of the seven IPA financial services papers that were able to reveal sufficient data, the average ROI of advertising was 79 per cent in the 12 months following.

This chapter has demonstrated no fewer than eight ways in which advertising contributes to a complex financial services sales process – one in which it is commonly said that products are sold, not bought. It is essential to consider advertising's manifold effects in this detail, because otherwise you cannot assess its impact on the costs and workings of the organisation. It is also extremely beneficial to an agency to acquire the grasp of the workings of a client's business that comes with this kind of analysis. The IPA Data Bank can provide considerable supporting evidence to build a similar advertising case in most markets and situations.

The argument in brief: Chapter 7

- 'Big ideas' are more valuable than advertising executions.
- There are four places to find a big idea:
    1 Product interrogation to reveal the product truth
    2 Consumer research to reveal a fresh insight
    3 Company culture audit to reveal brand positioning and values
    4 Corporate ambition audit to reveal a new market space.
- When advertising is developed to a genuinely big idea it has the power to positively influence and motivate a workforce.
- There are four ways in which a big idea can be applied to motivate a workforce:
    1 By raising morale
    2 Communicating a new direction
    3 Helping to build a strong company culture
    4 Helping to engineer change.

Chapter 7

How advertising motivates the workforce

Johnny Hornby

Finding and utilising a big idea in advertising to motivate the workforce

One of the things that hampers agencies' ability to get the credit we should for doing the work we do is that we call ourselves advertising agencies. Advertising agencies produce advertising. Good agencies produce good advertising. Good advertising has the power to raise awareness and create consideration and this in turn helps to increase sales. In fact many agencies nowadays help to further this very limited understanding by agreeing to contracts with clients where the bonus element is calculated on the basis of the advertising campaign's ability to increase either or both. In some cases there is also a variable that includes a sales-related element, but others find this too difficult to attribute directly to the advertising. Rarely is an agency remunerated or judged on any other measures attributed to the effect of the advertising.

Yet when advertising agencies are good they produce more than advertising campaigns. When they are good they produce ideas, and when they are really good they create big ideas.

What is a big idea?

A big idea is an idea that makes a difference. A big idea can drive a company or brand in all kinds of categories to extraordinary levels of achievement well beyond the limits of an awareness index. How do you define the size of an idea? By the size of the difference it makes.

Big ideas are more important and potentially much more valuable than advertising executions, and the happy coincidence is that where advertising executions are developed to a big idea they tend to be better and much longer lasting. Beyond that, the effect of a big idea communicated through advertising can and should be measured by more than simply increases in awareness, consideration or even sales – a big advertising idea can generate valuable PR, change perceptions in the City, it can sell merchandise, create a number-one single and one particularly valuable dimension is the effect that advertising can have when it is amplifying the big idea driving an organisation. That is how advertising can motivate the workforce.

Let us take the example of Tesco's 'Every Little Helps' campaign, a fantastic long-running advertising campaign of more than 8 years. It performs brilliantly against any criteria one would traditionally judge advertising by, it won an IPA Effectiveness Grand Prix for its ability to effect sales and consideration, and a Cannes Grand Prix for its creativity. But 'Every Little Helps' is much more than an advertising campaign, it's a big idea. It tells you how to behave if you work at Tesco (and indeed running the advertising campaign at Tesco is referred to as 'informal training'), it helps you with your new product development, it provides the backdrop for cause-related marketing initiatives such as 'Computers for Schools' and presents an image to the City and shareholders that shows an organisation that is in touch with its customers and the nation.

When advertising's role is that of amplifying the big idea we should be measuring more than the sales and the Millward Brown, we should be analysing the organisation's ability to do things before and after the advertising, the morale of that company, the strength of, or changes in its culture as a result of advertising, or even the ability of the company to change when inspired by a big idea through advertising.

In short, advertising a big idea has the ability to motivate a workforce in the following ways:

1 By raising morale
2 Communicating a new direction
3 Helping to build a strong company culture
4 Helping to engineer change.

In order to do any of the above, however, the advertising has to contain a genuinely big idea – a media infinite thought which too few campaigns contain.

Four places to find a big idea

Many people in marketing communications and agencies talk about big ideas, but very few produce them. A very good agency may have 25 brands and at best only three or four genuinely big ideas.

The truth is that big ideas don't grow on trees, and while there may be one or two in the history of big ideas that came out of the blue, the likelihood is that they are to be found by careful research and creative thinking and the answer will emerge from one of four areas:

1 Product interrogation to reveal the product truth
2 Consumer research to reveal a fresh insight
3 Company culture audit to reveal brand positioning and values
4 Corporate ambition audit to reveal a new market space.

Over the years different areas have come in and out of fashion as sources for big ideas but all big ideas will have emerged from one of these areas, and in truth whether in or out of fashion all four remain valid areas for investigation.

Product truth

In the good old days you 'interrogated the product until it confessed to its truth' as I think Robin Wight both preached and demonstrated with BMW. And while the other three areas have come more into fashion since, USPs can still be used to carve out extraordinary growth in mature and cluttered markets. The Stella Artois idea of being worth the sacrifice is a good example of this, as was the launch of Goldfish with the notion of being 'surprisingly practical'. A good old-fashioned product truth (Stella is slightly more expensive; a credit card that gives you money off your gas bill) leading to a genuinely big idea that not only delivered strong and effective advertising and communications, but also provided a strong template for product development and new product extensions in the very cluttered credit card market.

It may not be fashionable to hunt for USPs nowadays, but although they are harder to find than 20 years ago they still have the potential to form the basis of a big idea.

A fresh consumer insight

'Every Little Helps' is a great example of this. The battleground in supermarket retailing used to be between those who offered quality and those who offered value. The focus was on the products and brands you sold, yours were either better quality brands or you had a wider range of brands or your products were better value, or cheaper – if you didn't mind putting it that way.

Tesco found a fresh consumer insight. Life is not always a bed of roses, and shopping can be a big contributor to that – whether you are a mum with three kids to cart around the supermarket on a wet Wednesday in November or a bloke that couldn't care less what country the grapefruit comes from or what Delia says you can do with it. So anything that makes shopping that little bit easier makes life that little bit better. That's much more than an advertising idea, it's an idea to take a lacklustre number two and to turn it into Britain's biggest and most successful retailer – initially communicating a new direction to staff, then raising morale and over time contributing to a unique and well-defined company culture.

Fresh consumer insights like these can often be those that are best found by approaching a category or sector from afar, a look at a company or brand's existing research might unearth something without having to commission any new research. In particular looking afresh at the parts of the research that are often overlooked like the first twenty minutes of the focus group where people tend to discuss their relationship with and attitudes towards a sector which can often be key to unlocking a fresh approach.

The company culture

The argument this chapter seeks to make is that finding a genuinely big idea and then communicating it, has the added benefit of being able to motivate a workforce, and as a part of that to help shape a corporate culture. Interestingly perhaps, that big idea can in fact originate from a corporate culture or set of beliefs for a corporate body in the first place.

While product truths and consumer insights were for many years the main-stays of brand thinking, the company culture has emerged since the 1980s as a powerful source of big ideas for companies and brands such as Apple, Virgin, and Nike. It is probably not a coincidence in these instances that these compa-nies had very strong and visionary leaders with a passion to tell their story.

It is from a thorough investigation of how a company works, what it believes in, what its values are and how it behaves that one can find the inspiration for a big idea. Steve Jobs doesn't believe that Apple are in the business of making boxes to help people get their jobs done, he doesn't believe in grey computers or computers as mundane tools to make us more efficient. Steve Jobs believes that 'the people who believe they can change the world are the ones who probably do'. He believes in thinking differently and appeals to those of us that like to think we are more creative than others (or at least that is what we would like others to believe about us). To produce 'Tools for creative minds' is what Apple believe they get up in the morning and go to work to do, a big idea that motivates the consumer in advertising but also the existing or indeed prospective workforce.

The same could be said of Virgin's 'consumer champion' positioning, creating the perception that there are hundreds of clever young things wearing jeans and turning markets that aren't currently operating in the interests of the consumer on their head for the benefit of the customer. A powerful idea for consumers, a powerful notion also if you are needing to rapidly create a strong corporate culture in a fledgling new business which is often the case with Virgin start-ups. Virgin businesses are very separate businesses in many cases, with Richard Branson and his small team and the brand name being the only common link. The big idea of 'championing the consumer' that is so often applied to a Virgin business would make you feel these disparate teams were peas out of the same pod.

Corporate ambition to reveal new market space

The most contemporary perhaps of the four sources of a big idea is the notion that it can be found by defining a corporate ambition for a company or brand that then reveals a new market space.

It may seem years ago now, but the AA's '4th emergency service' remains one of the best examples of how interrogating and understanding the corporate ambitions of an organisation can provide the insight for defining a new market space. The AA had been in the roadside assistance market, and HHCL reclassified the company as the '4th emergency service'. The resulting advertising and communications are well recognised for their potency, but the big idea was more powerful than simply the stimulant for effective TV and DM campaigns. The AA employee was one day a roadside assistance guy and the next day he was part of a team who were – to their members – the '4th emergency service'. There can be few more motivating repositionings as far as the workforce is concerned and having that big idea amplified to the nation so not only is your job elevated but everyone you know knows it too.

Many agencies lament their disenfranchisement and exclusion from the top client table nowadays, but this rich source of big ideas requires that a foot is put back in the door with a genuine interrogation of what the company wants to achieve at the highest and loftiest level and it is from there that a '4th emergency service' has the potential to emerge (see Figure 7.1).

Having found the big idea you can then use it not only to inform an advertising campaign (that should do all the good things ad campaigns do) in terms of awareness, consideration and sales but also potentially to help you motivate the workforce in the four ways I outlined earlier. More often than not, however, advertising is not consciously deployed in order to motivate the workforce, it

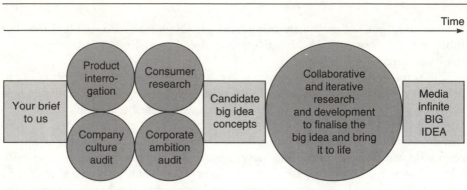

Figure 7.1 Where to find a big idea

just so happens that big ideas communicated through advertising have delivered that effect. Were you to start with the aim of using a big idea to motivate your workforce, working out what change you wanted to effect in advance should make it easier to narrow down where to look for your big idea. For example, where you to want to use advertising to communicate a change of direction and positioning to your workforce you would be most likely to be looking in the corporate ambition area.

Using a big advertising idea to raise company morale

The famous British Airways repositioning is a classic example of this. A demoralised workforce was very much a part of the airline's early 1980s failure. In 1981/1982 it was a company running at a loss of £541 million and rated among the least attractive of the prospective privatisation targets. Hand in hand with staff training 'The World's Favourite Airline', a big idea born out of a very clever spin on a product truth, motivated BA staff and set expectations for the way they should behave. From the day that campaign aired the people working for the airline no longer were the employees of a beleaguered and behind-the-times organisation, they worked for 'The World's Favourite Airline' and could stand proud as members of a team that deserved to be the envy of the industry. Similarly motivating ideas have been developed out of the product truths associated with being in the police force, being a teacher and indeed the Army with 'Be the best'. While all these campaigns were developed as recruitment advertising ideas – the public statement of the product truth worked as a highly motivating reminder of why the individuals already employed in these intrinsically, rather than extrinsically, motivating professions had chosen to do what they did.

Communicating a new direction

The low point in the recent history of the Labour Party was the 1983 conference, old Labour's stand resulting in the defection of those in the centre right to form the SDP. It was from that low point that the modernisers and creators of what would become New Labour set about trying to rebuild and then subsequently make the party electable.

In essence, the big idea that the party was rebuilt around can be found in the area of new market space. The corporate ambition was to create a modern and relevant social democratic party based around the big idea of 'equality of opportunity'. Old Labour, by contrast, had concentrated on trying to create an 'equality of outcome'. The poor get richer and the richer get poorer and we all end up in a fairer place in the middle. The big idea of New Labour removed for people the difficult choice between the head and the heart, the emotional and rational. You can be in favour of helping out those whose life chances are more limited than yours and you can vote to enhance those with the contribution your taxes make to the state without having to sacrifice your own ambitions. New Labour was about the politics of 'and' rather than the politics of 'or'. This change was fundamental to ensure that voters could reassess the party as an electable option. The big idea of New Labour and the communication of it through advertising and all forms of communication crystallised the change.

Beyond the electorate, though, New Labour was an idea that motivated and mobilised the Labour Party itself to believe that they could again be members of an organisation that could govern, that had the chance to make a change in Britain. 'New Labour' galvanised the party to work harder and longer in the wake of the defeat in 1992 and played a big part not only as a motivator but also as a very clear means of communicating to all supporters and members what it was that the party now stood for. The big idea of New Labour has informed advertising in the form of party political broadcasts, posters and print for many years now – much of which has been as much about motivating party activists and workers as it has been about influencing voter behaviour. 'A lot done, a lot more to do', for example, was a campaign aimed at communicating the party's sense of purpose and mission in government to the electorate, but also aimed at keeping the party motivated and focused on how much hard work lay ahead for the party now it was in power. 'Get out and vote or this gets in' may appear to be a trite joke at first glance but was designed to wake up those party members who felt that the 2001 election was a foregone conclusion to the consequences that their apathy could result in. It was this that enabled party workers, activists and supporters to simply articulate both the change from the Labour Party of the past and genuine difference between New Labour and the Tories.

Peter Mandelson puts it very simply: 'The big idea of "New Labour" motivated party workers and followers because it gave them the idea that there was a chance of winning, there's all the motivation you need for a team or group.'

Advertising a big idea to help build a strong company culture

From the day he opened his first shop Charles Dunstone began creating a company culture that was entirely focused on the customer. To this day he and his team remain obsessed with developing a business and culture that is entirely focused on giving the customer what they want.

From the beginning of the boom in mobile phones The Carphone Warehouse positioned itself as a brand that stood between the consumer and the confusing world of the handset manufacturers and airtime providers. 'Simple, Impartial Advice' acted as a powerful and motivating statement for the many who found this new world complicated and frightening. As a big idea it drove fantastic growth in the business but every time an ad came on the radio it not only confirmed the brand's point of view in the mind of the consumer, it also acted as a reminder to every member of the company of what the organisation was about and how it was to behave with its customers.

Helping to engineer change

As the mobile marketplace has moved towards saturation so there has been a need for The Carphone Warehouse to evolve its big idea. 'For a better mobile life' recognises that the marketplace and the relationship that customers will want with the brand will be longer term. That the relentless focus on the customer isn't just about when they buy a phone, it's about understanding the role that the phone plays in their lives and the potential that increasingly new mobile phone technologies will have to make people's mobile lives easier. In essence the role of The Carphone Warehouse is no longer as a shop that sells mobile phones, the role of the brand is as a service to people in their mobile lives.

Translating this change in advertising was a vital part of meeting the challenge of this changing marketplace, but the 'For a better mobile life' idea encapsulates more than a consumer proposition. The advertising succeeds in demonstrating to The Carphone Warehouse sales consultants that it isn't the phone that people choose that is important, but where they get it from, because a phone supported by The Carphone Warehouse will have a 'happier and more productive life'. Advertising in this instance works as a backdrop for the internal communications and rigorous training that The Carphone Warehouse invest in, but it is an important and valuable magnifier to help engineer the adoption of an evolution of a big idea.

Advertising containing a genuinely big idea has the ability to positively affect a lot more than the traditional measures associated with advertising. Motivating a workforce is one that many agencies and clients have subsequently discovered to be particularly powerful.

Thorough investigation of a company's or brand's product, consumer, company culture and corporate ambition not only gives you the best chance of finding the insight for a big idea but also gives you a better understanding of that company or brand than sometimes agencies have when they investigate only the product and consumer areas. This greater understanding has further benefits. It puts you in a better position to recognise a big idea when you come across it and to recognise the potential it may have outside of simply influencing advertising and communications. With that insight we could be better positioned to know how we want to apply the idea to motivate the workforce in different ways, to raise morale, to help build a strong culture or indeed to communicate a change of direction.

If you are still unsure ask yourself this. Would you rather work for Nike or Adidas? PlayStation or Nintendo? Apple or Compaq?

The argument in brief: Chapter 8

- Advertising is one part of the marketing mix. Though it can also build the value of the brand on a company's balance sheet[1], it traditionally supports the revenue aspect of the business plan by helping to acquire new customers and encouraging existing ones to stay and spend more.
- Online advertising, however, can play a role not only in sales, but also in distribution and cost-reduction, thus demonstrating multiple business effects.
- Online advertising is a highly measurable/accountable medium for both driving sales and increasing awareness.
- To optimise the contribution that online can make, a company needs to:
  - View online as both a marketing channel and a channel-to-market
  - Be clear on the objectives of using online
  - Involve the company's senior business planners in key online initiatives
  - Be open to non-traditional and, by definition, unfamiliar media.

Chapter 8

How online advertising can produce measurable business effects

Charlie Dobres

Introduction

Online advertising is an entire marketing toolkit just waiting to be used. It is probably better in fact to talk in terms of online *marketing* as the digital arena lends itself to direct marketing, PR, advertising, distribution, new product development, creating a website and more. Ironically, given that most marketers already therefore know 90 per cent of what they need to know to venture online, the greatest barrier to usage is still fear of the unknown.

More than 50 per cent of the UK population is now online[2]. All demographic and psychographic groups are there, as are all levels of business people – 91 per cent of the UK's top 4 per cent of earners are now online, 33 per cent of them 'logging on' every day.[3]

So, it is important to at least be aware of the multi-faceted way in which online, interactive media can reach an audience, enhance a campaign's effectiveness and contribute directly to the bottom line. Indeed, online advertising can produce measurable results both offline (in shops) and online (via websites). Where retailers have put measures in place, a ratio of up to £7 spent in-store for every £1 of on online advertising has been noted.[4] So, online advertising can drive sales, but equally it can promote awareness and help to build brand.[5] Increasing numbers of studies have shown that an online ad can actually achieve similar brand recall to a television commercial.[6]

So, what questions do marketing people ask themselves when considering whether to use online media in their marketing mix?

'I'm not risking getting involved in an area about which I know bugger all'

It's worth addressing this issue first. Online seems to polarise opinion and reaction among marketers. Many took the plunge at a time when the world economy was in good shape. Using new media at that time felt less risky, even progressive. But deciding to use new media in times of economic uncertainty requires more head than heart, and this chapter seeks to provide a starting point. One thing that 'going online' does not require, however, is a whole new set of skills.

The good news is that 90 per cent of what you need to know, you already know.

The usual laws of advertising apply. Great online advertising is based on consumer insight, a compelling proposition, a motivating offer, a rewarding creative execution, put in front of the right audience at the right time – just like *normal* advertising. The key difference is that consumers can act immediately on the advertising through the same channel they viewed it.

Anyway, it's not *you* that you need to worry about; it's your colleagues. Companies that plan online advertising most effectively and handle responses most efficiently have addressed internal organisation issues that can act as a barrier. They have streamlined internal communications or even done away with outdated departmental divisions so as to enable sharing of consumer knowledge and speedy response to opportunities and threats. For example, an online advertising campaign/promotion may elicit hundreds of email entries, among which may be some invaluable insights or even spontaneous feedback/complaints. But if the data is not seen and acted on quickly by the Customer Service team, then an opportunity may have been lost to retain an existing customer or win a new one. One answer to this would, of course, be to not put a 'comments' field on the entry form (or not run the promotion at all). However, as all marketers will know, a complaint unexpressed will be most likely to lead to a customer lost.

There can also be conflicting internal goals that prevent the optimum use of online. A not untypical one is where the online advertising activity leads to a sales uplift offline, in the company's shops. Unfortunately, there is a separate online budget which has to justify itself online, i.e. only the payback from online sales is counted. So, the online advertising manager has no incentive to drive the company's overall sales and, consequently, his or her objectives are out of line with the company's. If you think of the website as just another shop/branch, the irrationality of this approach is clear.

'Online is still in its infancy. Call me in 5 years' time'

No, the medium has actually become very advanced; inevitably, it is people's thinking that has lagged behind. The audience reach, targeting capability and overall accountability of online advertising have all reached maturity:

Audience reach

- 24 million people now use the web in the UK.[7]
- There are many broad reach sites (portals) that compare well with traditional media (see Figure 8.1).[8]
- For most of the day, from 8 am to 5 pm, the web now has a greater reach than TV among the key 25–34-year-old audience.[9] Smart fmcg companies that exploit this new balance of media consumption can reach audiences at relatively low cost, but with high accountability.

Targeting and accountability

- **Customers can be identified according to areas of interest, in a cost-effective way.** There are hundreds of sites which cater for any given area of interest. Central adserving (see below) and relatively low production costs mean that a campaign can be run across a large number of specialist sites and results easily gathered.
- **Adservers automatically supply all copy to websites as the viewer looks at the page.** It is this technology that allows you to dictate variables such

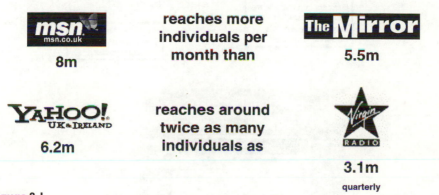

Figure 8.1

as; frequency of viewing; time of day; day of week; visibility by country (Figure 8.2).

- **Customers can be targeted according to how far down the acquisition path they are**. Pop-up boxes, banners, full-page ads and so on can be effective at grabbing the attention of those who are only at the awareness stage of purchase. At the other end of the scale, where customers have decided on a purchase and are looking for a supplier, they can be shown specific ads in response to typing in a keyword in a search engine.

'I'll have absolutely no idea if it's money well spent or not'

Lord Leverhulme would have loved online advertising. He could have found out quickly and cheaply exactly which half of his advertising was working.

Until recently, almost all online campaigns were measured solely on clickthrough[10]. Whilst this is a broad indicator of the response to a campaign, it doesn't tell you whether anyone went on to take any further action such as registering interest or even buying your product. Since 1999, however, technology has enabled the advertiser to 'tag' every person who is exposed to or responds to an ad, placing a small and unique piece of code known as a 'cookie'[11] on their computer. When that person subsequently makes a purchase, the cookie is read and the purchase value attached to that record.

Even if the customer doesn't make a purchase straight away, you can continue to track them until they do. In this way, online advertising is unique in its ability to directly measure campaign effectiveness by business-centric measures as well as traditional media-centric ones – a level of accountability that is clearly of great interest when advertising budgets are under pressure (see Figure 8.3).

This same approach means that a campaign can be tracked as it is running and changes made in order to optimise its performance – this is known as

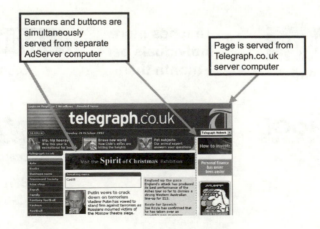

Figure 8.2

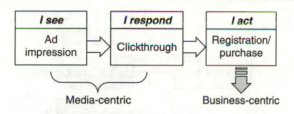

Figure 8.3

'fixing'. Indeed, many advertisers choose to run their online activity as a piece of ongoing marketing rather than as individual campaigns. Using the techniques described above, the marketer can build up a long-term picture of online marketing effectiveness.

'But I don't sell my product online'

For some companies, the Internet is an end-to-end opportunity. An insurance firm can generate awareness online, encourage enquiries and even complete the transaction. There are hundreds of examples where this happens across many sectors: airline tickets, books, toys, computers, lingerie, etc.

- 31 per cent of UK consumers have bought a product online.
- 26 per cent of them in the past three months.[12]

But companies that limit their online activity only to products that are available online are flying in the face of consumer behaviour. For example:

- More than 40 per cent of all UK consumers regularly research products online before making a purchase.[13]
- But with cars, for example, only 1.1 per cent of people go on to make the purchase online.[14]

So, just because the Internet *can* be a cost-effective distribution medium, its role in purchase decisions that are fulfilled offline (in shops/showrooms), should not be understated. Similarly, just because online is such a highly accountable direct response medium, that should not preclude its use in awareness and brand building.

In practice, a single online campaign will have multiple effects: It will attract some immediate response; some deferred response (when consumers have the time/inclination); and broad awareness, as with posters (Figure 8.4).

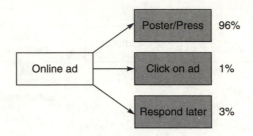

Figure 8.4

- Poster/press = Awareness building: Online ads are viewed on-screen from less than 2 feet away. They appear as 'mini posters' (banners) or as more interruptive formats that take up most of the screen.
- Respond later = Deferred Response: Typically, this represents around a 3 per cent response rate for every 1 per cent of Immediate Response. Because these people are responding when *they* are ready to, conversion rates to purchase tend to be significantly higher than from Immediate Responses.
- Click on ad = Immediate Response: Those people who are in the market for the product at the time or who are just curious. They may only get as far as the product's website homepage and go no further, but in this way they are acting like the person who takes a look inside a shop (perhaps several times) before buying anything.

Conclusion

'If it's so great, why isn't everybody using it?'

'I think there is a world market for maybe five computers.'
Thomas Watson, Chairman, IBM (1949)

'Television won't be able to hold on to any market it captures after the first six months. People will soon get tired of staring at a plywood box every night. '
Darryl F. Zanuck, 20th Century Fox – President (1946)

'This "telephone" has too many shortcomings to be seriously considered as a means of communication. The device is inherently of no value to us.'
Western Union (1876)

There is a gap. On one side of the equation, consumer uptake of the web and other digital media has reached mass-market proportions. More and more consumers are spending more and more time online and buying/researching more and more products. The statistics are clear and overwhelming. On the other side, some marketing practitioners are still reticent to use online advertising, other than experimentally, in their marketing mix.

The success or failure of online marketing is mostly dependent on the approach that marketers take to it rather than on any kind of inherent strengths or weaknesses of the medium. Appalling TV commercials do not undermine the overall power of television; cluttered, ill-thought-out posters do not leave us cursing the outdoor medium as a whole. So it is with the Internet and indeed all digital media, for it should be noted that online advertising now covers mobile phones (texting), interactive TV, e-mail marketing and even handheld computers.

Marketers are already sending people offers and inviting competition entries via sms text. Last-in-break interactive TV slots are now increasingly common on digital TV and sponsorships are available on the interactive pages 'behind' some major TV shows. Ads with pictures can be placed within opt-in e-mails and these can get high response rates. And offers can be downloaded onto people's handheld PDAs and they can e-mail back responses when they 'synchronise' their devices. All these techniques and more are now readily available.

People's media attention *is* fragmenting: 75 per cent of UK adults have a mobile phone and 52 per cent of 7–16 year olds.[15] Between these two groups, some 1.4 billion text messages are sent every month.[16] Among the 50 per cent of the UK households who now have a net connection, over 30 per cent say that they are watching less television as a consequence.[17] Is it any wonder that BARB figures show a 13.5 per cent drop in audiences across commercial TV?[18] Of course people are watching less TV, there are just so many more things to occupy people's time. So marketers have to follow them into the new media they are consuming in ever greater numbers. Follow them or risk losing their attention.

And online *is* different from other media – it offers at least one unique and crucial attribute. The consumer can go all the way from awareness to interest to desire to action, all within the same medium, even within the same session. When you add in the technological developments that enable reasonably straightforward tracking of this path, you are left with an advertising medium that not only *can* demonstrate a direct contribution to a company's bottom line, but often *does*.[19]

Postscript: 'How do I start?'

Some useful contacts:

IPA – Digital Marketing Group
Director for Media Affairs
020 7201 8203
www.ipa.co.uk

ISBA – New Media Group
Director of Media & Advertising Affairs
020 7499 7502
www.isba.org.uk

Internet Advertising Bureau (UK)
www.iabuk.net

AAR Digital
020 7612 1200
www.aargroup.co.uk

Notes

1. *Advalue*, 'How advertising affects shareholder value', Issue 5, February 2000.
2. Oftel, October 2002.
3. IPSOS-RSL 2001.
4. i-level Digital Partnerships research.
5. Internet Advertising Bureau: 'Banners build brands: four research studies provide conclusive proof' (www.iabuk.net) Research Archives).
6. Harris Interactive/Unicast, June 2001 (http://www.harrisinteractive.com/news/ allnewsbydate.asp?NewsID=321).
7. Oftel, October 2002.
8. September 2002, Nielsen//Netratings; Mirror Group; RAJAR.
9. Nielsen//NetRatings, BARB.
10. Clickthrough is the number of clicks on an online ad expressed as a percentage of the impressions the ad had. NB: It is *not* the equivalent of a DM response rate, as impressions are not the same as reach.
11. A cookie is a line of text that sits on your hard drive – this is what one looks like: SITESERVERID=3149B19C228AD411B81 F00902752105Bwww.ask.co. uk/0419572940829756627224079532829367857* (It cannot identify you by name, only by computer and thus is anonymous.)
12. Forrester Internet User Monitor.
13. Forrester Internet User Monitor.
14. Cap Gemini Ernst & Young, October 2001.
15. NOP January 2002.
16. Operator statements.
17. Forrester Internet User Monitor.
18. BARB January 2002.
19. IPA Effectiveness Awards 2000 (4 star winner) – easyJet online advertising campaign (www.ipa.co.uk).

The argument in brief: Chapter 9

- Firms that maintain or increase their advertising during a recession are able to gain market share at a significantly faster rate than when the market is expanding.
- Although this leads to a reduction in short-term financial performance, the resulting gain in market share should lead to a sustainable increase in the firm's return on investment.

Chapter 9

Advertising during a recession

Alex Biel and Stephen King

Defining recession

Bernard Baruch said that it's a recession when your neighbour is out of work (adding that when *you're* out of work it's a depression!).

Although the recessions that make the headlines are generally seen as all-encompassing and national in scope, this definition obscures the fact that 'normal' national economic conditions are really an averaging of good times in some industries, bad times in others; growth in some parts of the country and decline in others.

During a national recession everyone gets hurt; but some sectors feel the heat more than others. Conversely, during a period of expansion some markets reap greater benefits.

A more useful, empirically determined definition of recession is one which relates annual growth at one point in time to the longer-term growth trend of a *specific market*. The Center for Research & Development, in collaboration with the Strategic Planning Institute, has used this market-specific concept of recession to analyse consumer businesses in the Profit Impact of Market Strategy (PIMS) database. The PIMS database included, at the time of this analysis, 749 consumer businesses, with a minimum of four years' data covering those businesses and the markets in which they participate.[1]

The PIMS database is the only source that contains both marketing data and financial information for the same consumer-based businesses.

A working definition

For our purposes, a specific market is considered to be in recession when short-term growth *lags* long-term growth by at least four percentage points. On the other hand, when a market *exceeds* its long-term growth rate by more than four percentage points, we can say that it is in a period of expansion.[2] Using this definition, it is possible to describe how consumer businesses fare under different market conditions.

The relationship of changing market conditions

To understand what happens during changing market conditions, it is useful to look at *changes* in rates of return for those businesses enjoying market expansion compared to those suffering a shrinking market. As Figure 9.1 shows, there is a substantial market effect that impacts a firm's return on invested capital.

It is no great surprise to learn that when the market expands, the average consumer business in the PIMS database enjoys an increased return on investment. Indeed, one might expect rates of return to increase even more sharply during a period of market growth; the fact that they do not may be explained to some extent by the difficulty that some businesses face in meeting increased demand.

When a market contracts, on the other hand, the profits of the average business decline. In this study, the average business lost just under two percent-

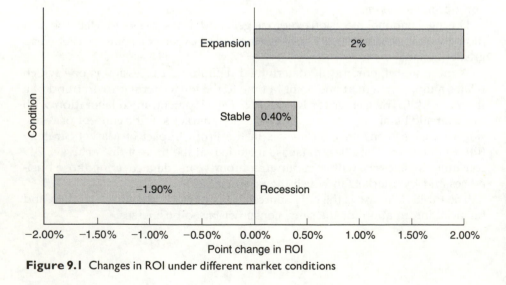

Figure 9.1 Changes in ROI under different market conditions

age points of profit, dropping from a return on investment of 21.9 per cent to 20.0 per cent.[3]

Changes in advertising spending related to changes in return on investment

What is the relationship of changes in advertising spending to changes in return on investment? To answer this question, we looked at the specific spending policies employed by the businesses in the database.

Of the 339 observations of the businesses that experienced recessionary periods, one-third cut their spending on advertising by an average of 11 per cent, while two-thirds actually spent at a *higher* rate than before.[4]

Of those businesses raising their advertising investment, the majority – 60 per cent – limited their increase to no more than 20 per cent more than they had previously been spending. The average business in this group increased spending by 10 per cent. However, the other 40 per cent of those businesses that raised their expenditures made *substantial* increases ranging from 20 per cent to 100 per cent, and averaging 49 per cent.

Table 9.1 shows how changes in return on investment relate to these changes in spending. Clearly, businesses suffer a reduction in return on investment whether spending is cut or increased during a recession. Indeed, businesses yielding to the natural inclination to cut spending in an effort to increase profits in a recession find that it doesn't work. These businesses fared no better in terms of return on investment than those which modestly increased their ad spending.

Those firms that *substantially* increased their advertising budgets experienced the largest drop in return on investment: a reduction of 2.7 percentage points. However, as we shall see, those advertisers who increase spending – whether modestly or aggressively – achieve greater market share gains than those who cut their advertising investment. This, in turn, puts them in a better position to increase profits after the recession.

Table 9.1 Changes in ROI related to changes in advertising spending during a recession

Spending	Changes in ROI
Decreased (ave −11%)	−1.6%
Modest increase (ave +10%)	−1.7%
Substantial increase (ave +49%)	−2.7%
Average change – all businesses (see Figure 9.1: Recession)	−1.9%

The links between market conditions, market share, and advertising

These findings led us to dissect the relationship between changes in return on investment and changes in advertising pressure.

As we showed in an earlier study,[5] advertising spending and return on investment are linked – but only indirectly. Advertising directly affects brand 'salience': it makes the advertised brand more top-of-mind among prospects. It also tends to amplify the relative perceived quality of the brand, which in turn increases the brand's perceived value for money. Salience and perceived quality drive buying behaviour, which of course is reflected in sales, and therefore in Share of Market (SOM). But market share is affected by market conditions as well as advertising pressure (Figure 9.2).

Here we see that the businesses in the PIMS database enjoy a *higher* rate of share growth during downturns, and a *lower* rate of share increase during stable periods and periods of growth.

One explanation for this is that weaker businesses – businesses with lower market shares – may be less able to defend themselves during downturns, while their larger competitors become more aggressive in order to partially make up sales that are threatened due to a lower growth rate of the total category. The PIMS database includes a broad range of consumer businesses; while some are strong and even market-dominating, others are less successful and weaker. However, on average, the businesses contributing data to PIMS are somewhat more likely to be the stronger players in their markets.[6]

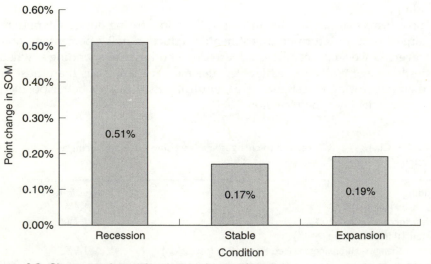

Figure 9.2 Changes in share related to market conditions

The relationship of advertising spending to market share

To identify the relationship of changes in spending to changes in share of market, we again analysed the data in terms of the spending strategies of the various businesses. As Figure 9.3 shows, those who reduced their budgets during recession attained much lower share gains than their more aggressive counterparts. On the other hand, marketers which increased spending were able to realise significant market share gains.

It is worth noting that, while there appear to be opportunities to win share by becoming increasingly competitive during a recession, when markets *expand*, share gains are harder to come by. This is demonstrated in Figure 9.4, which reveals the link between changing advertising investments and share as markets expand.

Marketers that decrease their spending during an expansion of the market lose share, albeit slightly; on average, they drop one-tenth of a share point. Those who increase their spending by upwards of 20 per cent as their market expands increase average share, but by only half a percentage point. In other words, the possibility of gaining share through increasing advertising appears to be greater when the total market is soft.

It is important to remember that the changes in both share of market and return on investment reported were achieved during the recession itself. Other research indicates that much – but by no means all – of the impact of advertising on sales is achieved in the year the budget is spent.[7] However, the main

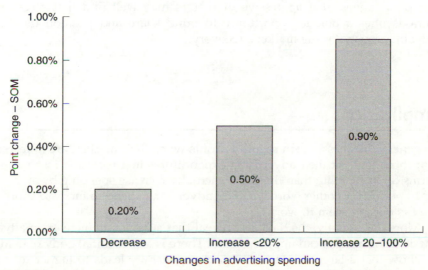

Figure 9.3 Changes in share related to changes in advertising spending during recession

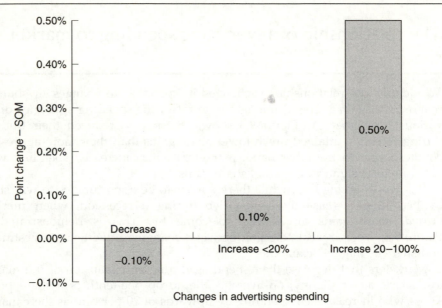

Figure 9.4 Changes in share related to changes in advertising spend during advertising

impact of share gains is translated into gains in profitability in subsequent periods.

While the data reported here are of course correlational, and do not necessarily prove causality, they nonetheless suggest that there may be some attractive share-building opportunities *during periods when business contracts*. Indeed, the data suggest that aggressive marketers may well find that recessionary periods offer a unique opportunity to build share and position themselves advantageously for the market's recovery.

Implications

In general, businesses earn reduced profits when their markets are in recession. But those that cut their advertising expenditures in a recession lose no less in terms of profitability than those who actually increase spending by an average of 10 per cent. In other words, cutting advertising spend to increase short-term profits doesn't seem to work.

More importantly, the data also reveal that a moderate increase in advertising in a soft market can improve share. There is a substantial body of evidence to show that a larger share of the market generally leads to higher return on investment.[8]

For the aggressive marketer, the data suggest that a more ambitious increase in expenditure, although reducing short-term profit, can take advantage of the opportunity afforded by a recession to increase market share even further.

The PIMS data indicate that consumer marketers increasing their spending by an average of 48 per cent during a recession win virtually double the share gains of those who increase their expenditures more modestly. While this aggressive increase in advertising is associated with a drop in return on investment of 2.7 per cent in the short term, it may nevertheless be acceptable to the marketer looking ahead to post-recession growth.[9]

Notes

1. Since each business unit contributed a minimum of four years of data, and since recessions and expansions were defined as deviations from the normal growth trend of the industry, a given business unit provided at least one, and often more than one observation. Thus the sample of 749 business units provided a total of 1639 observations.
2. For the purposes of this analysis, we define short-term periods as one year. Long-term trends of a market are defined as a minimum of four years.
3. Return on investment is calculated before taxes and interest charges for the purpose of this analysis.
4. Some businesses doubtless did take a clearly aggressive stance in light of the softness of the market. But it is probable that for other businesses in the sample spending was committed prior to the receipt of sales or market data. This helps explain why more businesses increased spending than curtailed their efforts.
5. 'The impact of advertising expenditures on profits for consumer businesses' (The Ogilvy Center for Research & Development, 1987).
6. Since the concept of share of market is a zero sum notion, it is important to note that the share of market averages described here relate to the businesses studied rather than shares of all the entrants in each of the specific markets involved.
7. See Reading 3 (Table 2 and Note 2).
8. See Note 5.
9. R. D. Buzzell and B. M. Gale, *The PIMS Principles*, The Free Press, 1987.

This chapter is adapted from *Options and Opportunities for Consumer Businesses: Advertising During a Recession*, Alexander L. Biel and Stephen King.
©**The WPP Center for Research & Development, October 1990**

PART C

Customer Effects

The argument in brief: Chapter 10

■ This chapter reviews some of the historical precepts that still govern much of our thinking about advertising to this day.
■ It challenges some of these views directly, and shows how recent thinking about longer and broader effects paints a very different picture of advertising's role in the twenty-first century.

The evolution of our thinking about 'how advertising works'

Tim Broadbent

The IPA Advertising Effectiveness Awards celebrated their twentieth anniversary in the millennium year 2000. It seems appropriate to review what they have achieved. What would our world be like if the Awards did not exist?

Consider the world in which they were launched. In the 1970s it was intellectually respectable to claim that it was impossible to prove that advertising works, which amounts to admitting it does not work.

For example, in 1973 a leading practitioner published a textbook called *The Business of Advertising*. He wrote, 'The effects of advertising are largely immeasurable...Advertising makes an unknown contribution to selling goods'.[1] The point was that many marketing activities other than advertising affect consumer demand for advertised brands, including price, packaging, merchandising and so on, as well as influences beyond marketing's control, such as competitive activity. Separating advertising effects from the mix seemed impossible.

But this lack of accountability is dangerous. A finance director might conclude that if advertising effects are so thoroughly swamped by other activities as to be 'immeasurable', they can only be small effects at best. Spending money on advertising could be seen as a leap of faith by the marketing department.

This was the context in which Simon Broadbent initiated a new kind of advertising competition. The objective was to create a collection of published case histories to show that research, properly used, could isolate what advertising had contributed over and above other elements in the mix, and that advertising was a contributor to profit, not just a cost.

Broadbent was thus setting himself in opposition, both to industry colleagues who said it was 'nonsense' to believe that ad effects could be isolated, and also to sections of the business community that believed advertising was bunk. It appears he was right and they were wrong. The Awards have become part of the settled order of things. But it is important to understand how controversial they were at the time.

There are now more than 700 case histories in the IPA Effectiveness Data Bank, covering almost every advertised category. All are available for inspection via the IPA website at www.ipa.co.uk. There is nothing in the world to match this body of learning, and the UK has become the global centre of excellence for evaluation. The cases show how effective individual campaigns were, providing performance benchmarks for agencies and clients, and they demonstrate general methods for isolating ad effects anybody can use.

The original goals have been achieved. No reasonable person, faced with this mountain of evidence, could claim that ad effects cannot be measured. Yet the Awards persist. Why? Because of the continuing fascination with what is meant by saying that an ad 'works'. The Awards have evolved as understanding of effectiveness has deepened.

The person in the street, or even the finance director in the boardroom, thinks an ad works when it sells more. We instinctively look for a return in terms of how many boxes leave the factory. In so doing, we unconsciously reflect a philosophy of advertising that is at least 80 years old.

Two books published in 1923 have dominated the way advertising has been evaluated: *The Principles of Advertising* by Daniel Starch (who founded what is said to be the first market research company in the same year, selling research techniques for ad evaluation that are still used), and *Scientific Advertising* by Claude Hopkins.[2] Both offered identical definitions of advertising: they said it is 'salesmanship in print'.

This does not only mean that advertising should be persuasive. Supermarkets did not exist, and many household products were distributed by armies of door-to-door salesmen. Direct response advertising was being defined as an alternative distribution channel. This point is easily forgotten nowadays as doorstep selling has declined, but Starch was explicit: 'Advertising would seem ultimately to be justified ... as an agency of fair and economic competition in the distribution of goods'. In effect, advertising effectiveness was defined in terms of distributive efficiency (rate of sale per ad, compared to rate of sale per salesman), rather than in terms of its contribution to the business, as the Awards now define it.

The reference to 'print' is revealing. Most newspapers in the United States were local, as they still are. Mass communication was in its infancy: 1923 saw the first 'sound on film' movie and the first transatlantic wireless radio broadcast, while commercial TV was a generation away. What became the standard model of advertising was in fact based on direct response ads in local press.

Most advertising today does not distribute goods. When a salesman arrives at the home, people can buy directly. But when an ad appears on TV, people cannot buy instantly. They can only buy the next time they go to the shops. Shops sell, ads predispose.

Yet when marketing arrived in Britain in the 1950s, travelling over from the USA and alighting at Newcastle with Procter & Gamble, this philosophy arrived too. It was godparent to the new medium of commercial television, even though few TV ads are direct response.

The cases in the early years of the Awards followed the standard model. They isolated advertising's effect on short-term volumes. But this did not reflect all the ways in which advertising can be a serious business proposition. A new Awards criterion was introduced in 1990. The search for 'longer and broader' effects had begun.

This showed foresight. Research in the 1990s using single-source and fused panel data showed that most ads do indeed 'sell' in the short term, but that the average short-term increase for brands with continuous support is too small to pay back profitably.[3] Judged by the direct response criterion, most money spent on advertising is wasted. The Awards had been celebrating atypical successes, rather than reflecting what most advertising does most of the time.

The 'longer and broader' Awards category invited authors to demonstrate brand-building effects. Advertising does not only cause boxes to leave the factory. It also differentiates brands, which creates loyal customers who are willing to pay a premium price. Brands are machines for delivering quality earnings at high margins. They can be worth many times more than a firm's tangible assets. Advertising's typical role of adding value had been neglected.

A new kind of evaluation emerged in response to the challenge. Rather than just considering the sales effect of a single ad, authors examined the 'longer' effects of years of investment in advertising. The returns can be extraordinary. Some papers estimated that adspend paid back twenty times over. Advertising 'worked', but in a different way from the short-term responses measured before.

A third development in the Awards took place in the late 1990s. Authors were encouraged to investigate advertising's 'manifold' (or 'broader') effects. Unlike other marketing communications such as direct mail, broadcast ads are overheard beyond the consumer target. Is this wasteful? Or does reaching non-consumer audiences bring unique benefits?

The Awards contain many examples of how profitable manifold effects can be. Most firms do not sell directly to end consumers but to intermediaries, such as retailers. Advertising's effect on intermediaries is shown to account for a third or more of its total return. Benefits are also shown among other important stakeholders, for example trade partners and the City. These additional sources of return are invisible to consumer research, but are real nonetheless.

Astronomy offers an analogy. People have studied the skies for millennia but observations were restricted to what could be seen with the naked eye. It was not until Galileo picked up his telescope that it became possible to discover the universe to be vastly bigger than had ever been imagined. Moreover, most stellar objects broadcast energy on wavelengths outside the spectrum of visible light. Today's astronomers use radio, ultraviolet, X-ray and gamma ray telescopes. New ways of looking have shown that there is more to see than human eyes could ever know.

Similarly, the Awards have shown that advertising can pay back in more ways than are dreamt of in the standard model. Hopefully, more advertising researchers will lift their eyes from the short term alone and develop new techniques that, like new kinds of telescopes, look broader and deeper. The authors have shown that advertising creates value in places where conventional research does not go.

As for the client community, research carried out in 1998 showed that 51 per cent of ISBA members said they found the Awards 'helpful in justifying marketing and advertising expenditure' (up from 29 per cent in 1994).[4] The message is getting through, but we need to keep working at it.

Another survey showed that finance directors still resolutely fail to see marketing as essential. In 1999, 83 per cent said it was quite or very difficult to measure the effectiveness of their marketing effort, and that if business costs were under pressure most would cut marketing and advertising budgets first.[5]

This reflects a lack of customer focus in the boardroom. Only one company in three transmits customer satisfaction scores to the board, although two in three measure it.[6] But it is disappointing to find the 1970s myth of 'immeasurability' still alive and well among the resource allocators.

To conclude, we might summarise the history of the Awards as the progressive revelation of advertising's effects. Their lasting achievement has been to prove that it is possible to isolate advertising's influence. Advertising expenditure can be placed in the 'accountable' category rather than the 'immeasurable' category if the will to carry out evaluation exists.

Second, they have shown that a comprehensive assessment of advertising's return should include not only sales, but also brand-building and manifold effects (such as commanding a premium price and winning intermediaries' support).

The Awards have stimulated new thinking about what advertising does for clients, and encouraged new ways to measure and evaluate its effects. The work continues, but the marketing and advertising worlds would have been poorer without them.

References

1. Jones, R., *The Business of Advertising*. Longman, 1973.
2. Starch, D., *The Principles of Advertising*. Chicago, 1923. Hopkins, C., *Scientific Advertising*. New York, 1923.
3. Roberts, A. 'Advertising's short term effects', *Admap*, 359, 1996. Jones, J. P., *When Ads Work*, Lexington Books. 1995.
4. *IPA Monitor of advertising effectiveness*, IPA, 1998.
5. *Finance Directors survey*, IPA, 2000.
6. Ambler, T., *Marketing and the Bottom Line*, Pearson Education, 2000.

The argument in brief: Chapter 11

Relative retention explains profits better than market share, scale, cost position, or any other of the other variables usually associated with competitive advantage. (Bain & Co., quoted in *The Loyalty Effect*, Reichheld)

The value of loyal customers is being increasingly recognised. What is often less apparent is how loyalty is gained and cultivated and the potentially crucial role that advertising has to play in fostering it.

Some of the many benefits, which can affect any business and which impact at a corporate as well as at brand level are outlined below:

- Greater future certainty – business plans can predict sales and profits with a higher level of confidence.
- More realistic brand valuation – putting a worth on likely *future* performance and probable ability to defend against new market entries or competitive initiatives.
- Cost of customer management – more loyal customers make the business easier to administer. The relative costs of obtaining new customers against servicing old ones range from five- to twenty-fold, depending on the market category. Repeat purchasers need to be told less and are more forgiving of service lapses or failures.
- Quicker take-up of a new variant or range extension by virtue of having a ready-made purchase base.

Chapter 11

How advertising affects customer loyalty

Andrew Crosthwaite

The forces lined up against loyalty

In most markets the trend is to less close ties between the consumer and brands. Indeed, arguably, when we talk about brand relationships, we should refer to brand acquaintanceships. The growth of *individuality* means that to stick rigidly to the same choice can carry pejorative associations – buying the same marque of car, going on holiday to the same destination.

The plethora of *range extensions* in most fmcg markets means that the segmentation of needs is matched by a growth of options, making purchase patterns more repertoire driven – the varieties of toothpaste have increased five-fold in the last 10–15 years. In Table 11.1, the penetration of randomly

Table 11.1 The penetration of randomly selected leader brands between 1992 and 1997

Category	Penetration 1992	Penetration 1997
Breakfast cereal	43%	34%
Sun tan lotion	24%	20%
Household cleaner	40%	29%
Toilet tissue	48%	42%

Source: Target Group Index BMRB International

selected brand leaders is compared between 1992 and 1997. In nearly every case, not only had the user base fallen, but so had the proportion of users having it as their 'most often' brand.

Ironically, marketeers drive experimentation and then bemoan declining loyalty. This is at the heart of the paradox of wanting everyone else's customers to be promiscuous whilst our own remain committed.

Brand shift not switch

Because most markets operate on a repertoire basis, changes in behaviour tend to be the result of small changes over a long term.

Shifts in preference will come from:

- lack of availability (inconvenient and a subtle sign that a brand is less 'current')
- loss of confidence in performance characteristics
- the lure of 'newness' from a rival
- price changes in the market

and be characterised by:

- repeat trial of an alternative (often sporadic)
- changes in share of purchase over time

but also influenced by:

- whether the change is high or low risk (financial, time, reputation) mood and occasion (see Figure 11.1).

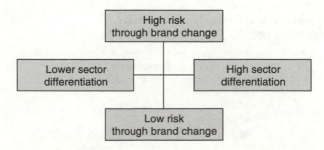

Figure 11.1 Mapping the risk of loyalty erosion

How can we measure loyalty?

Share of category purchase or usership is one obvious approach and for many companies is the only measure used. A loyalty measure that is purely derived from sales may mask some unpalatable truths and be no guide to future performance, or worse, actively misleading. In the 1970s, it was possible for an Italian car marque to have a very high level of repurchase ('loyalty'). In fact, corrosion problems had resulted in such poor resale value that the only way to be able to afford a new car was to trade in to the same franchise.

Many financial services customers are outwardly loyal in their behaviour, but are extremely dissatisfied. It tends to be only the perceived hassle of changing provider or a belief that 'they are all the same' that prevents defection. In fact, a fifth of a bank's customers may be attitudinally more positive about a bank other than the one they currently bank with. Indeed in this market, customers *actively* seek multiple relationships to avoid putting all their nest eggs in one basket, having three to four different companies on average with whom they bank, save, have a mortgage, pension, etc.

Even in a conservative market like this, disruption can be savage when a compelling product is offered in an innovative way. In 1996 and 1997 First Direct gained a 25 per cent share of all current accounts moved, despite only having 2 per cent of the total market. What can be assumed is that a brand can be vulnerable to competitive initiative when there are insufficiently strong foundations of goodwill or emotional affinity or belief to fall back onto.

Defining true loyalty

'True loyalty' goes beyond mere behavioural loyalty. It is a measure of the degree of closeness and affinity that customers feel towards brands or companies. This can be assessed in a number of ways (see Figure 11.2). This model

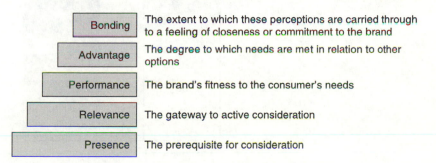

Bonding	The extent to which these perceptions are carried through to a feeling of closeness or commitment to the brand
Advantage	The degree to which needs are met in relation to other options
Performance	The brand's fitness to the consumer's needs
Relevance	The gateway to active consideration
Presence	The prerequisite for consideration

Figure 11.2 The Brand Dynamics Pyramid. *Source*: Adapted from Millward Brown

has been developed by Millward Brown, based on survey questions which allow the measurement of brand strength and weaknesses at different levels of consumer involvement:

- Presence is the prerequisite for consideration
- Relevance of proposition is a gateway to active consideration
- Performance is an assessment of the brand's fitness to the consumer's needs
- Advantage is the degree to which these needs are met in relation to other options in the repertoire (obviously this will vary according to mood and occasion)
- Bonding is the extent to which these perceptions are carried through to a feeling of closeness or commitment to the brand
- Bonded consumers may only be a small proportion of a brand's customer base – but they are likely to represent a high proportion of the brand's revenue. Figure 11.3 shows the proportion of total revenue accounted for by the bonded consumers in four UK packaged goods categories – tea, coffee, yellow fats and toothpaste.

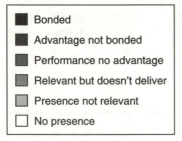
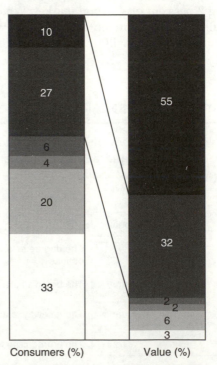

Consumers (%)   Value (%)

Figure 11.3 Attitudinal profile and value generated. Adapted from Millward Brown

Principal findings from Brand Dynamics and Brandbuilder

- Brands which gain share over time are likely to be those which currently have more than their fair share of bonded customers (see Figure 11.4).
- Brands which draw a high proportion of their sales from consumers at presence only and don't feel the brand has any particular advantages – rational, emotional or saliency based will:
  - suffer in the marketplace
  - work hard to justify a price premium
  - be vulnerable to the successful activity of their competitors.

It is possible to calculate whether for its size, familiarity and relevance, a brand has more than its fair share at each level of the pyramid. Similar principles are demonstrated by 'Brandbuilder', a model developed by The NPD Group in the USA (see Figure 11.5), which segmented 4000 buyers across 27 brands into three levels of purchase loyalty levels:

- high loyals
- moderate loyals
- low loyals/non-buyers.

A year later, 60 per cent of the high loyals who also demonstrated a *high attitudinal loyalty* to the brand were still loyal buyers, while only 25 per cent of those with the same level of purchase behaviour, but a *lower attitudinal* level for it were. Two groups were defined: 'Prospects', whose attitudes to the brand

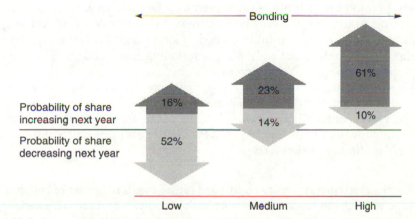

Figure 11.4 A proven link between consumer equity based on bonding levels and changes in market share. *Source*: Millward Brown

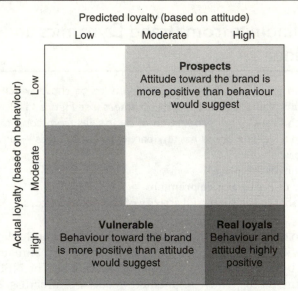

Figure 11.5 Attitudinal and behavioural loyalty model. *Source*: The NPD Group

are stronger than their behaviour; 'Vulnerables', whose behaviour is more committed than their attitudes. In two thirds of cases, where a brand had more 'Vulnerables' than 'Prospects', share went down year on year; where more 'Prospects' than 'Vulnerables', share had gone up.

Advertising in the context of other communication

Where promotional activity is often seen as a tangible tool, working hard and producing results (or not, as the case may be), the role of advertising as a loyalty driver can often be undervalued. 'Good general advertising can shape a brand's personality, but only direct marketing can build on-going, durable relationships.' (*Source*: Wunderman)

However, many of the widely recognised benefits of an effective advertising campaign impact *directly* onto customer loyalty and hence onto brand performance, brand profitability and brand value. There are many ways of increasing *behavioural* loyalty of consumers. However, price and other promotional activity have a number of downsides:

■ Functional attributes tend to be changed rather than a richer set of beliefs or associations which can sustain a long-term shift of choice – payback is limited.
■ Loyalty is generated to a price point or promotional mechanic, rather than to real or perceived brand benefits.

- 'Loyalty schemes' work only by delivering a benefit tangibly preferable to the competitive offer *and* relevant to the core of the brand offer. 74 per cent of adults own at least one loyalty card, with a quarter possessing three or more.
- AGB's Superpanel indicates that around a third of all supermarket card holders are no more than 'weakly loyal' to the store in question and although card holders make more frequent trips on the whole, they do not actually spend more than non-card holders. (In other words, customers have been given money for doing something that they were already doing.)

Advertising and the creation of attitudinal loyalty

Bonding and affinity are driven by a variety of factors, and their relative importance varies from category to category. However, many studies indicate that advertising can have a key role in developing these vital areas:

- Perceived product superiority – it is increasingly difficult for a brand to establish *and* sustain a genuine product-based advantage. However, advertising has the power to shape, channel and enhance consumers' perceptions of a brand's delivery.
- Emotional affinity with the brand – this transformation of product perceptions is one of advertising's most powerful effects, empirically evident in blind versus branded product tests. Advertising is almost unique in its ability to establish personalities and positioning for brands. These may enhance the usage experience, but they also provide the hooks that enable consumers to feel that a brand is emotionally 'the one for them'.
- High regard and status – advertising is also a powerful force for building and maintaining the status of the brand in the marketplace.

Importantly this goes beyond the immediate target of the communication in many cases. One of the critical measures of a brand's status is its *desirability* outside the immediate user base. Advertising is often criticised by advocates of narrower communication for its 'wastefulness'. However, it is the halo effect created by its ubiquity which can lead to enhanced valuation of a brand in the eyes even of those who, for example, could never afford it.

Loyalty is transactional – it has to be earned. Unless the customer embarks on a long-term relationship in a motivated frame of mind, it is likely to turn into a shallow relationship, characterised by sporadic one-off encounters. A critical aspect of driving brand preference (ultimately the engine of loyalty and brand strength), is the complex pattern of beliefs that consumers will have. And just as no two individuals are ever alike, so the impressions of brands that live inside peoples' minds differ. Innovatively expressed brand propositions through advertising media are a uniquely powerful way of generating these beliefs and impressions through a *shared experience* of a company or brand.

It is this process of creating customer closeness, through involvement and a belief in the superiority, that creates real brand differentiation.

The suggestion is not that advertising is the only way to build a committed franchise, but by laying the foundations and interacting with other elements of the marketing plan, highly effective and cost-efficient results can be generated. Figures 11.6–11.8 give evidence from the IPA Data Bank, a collection of case histories spanning two decades, which show clear examples of some of these principles in practice.

Summary and conclusions

The benefits of customer loyalty can be traced straight through to the balance sheet. Loyalty levels are a measure of both the current and long-term health of the brand. This is vital for more than just marketeers. Arguably it is the responsibility of every chief executive or financial director to look to these indicators, not just the duty of Marketing to evaluate them.

Loyalty is a complex subject. People are not disposed to be loyal in any aspect of their lives and their brand usage is no different. In fact market forces positively reward and promote loose and uncommitted brand ties. The result is that the marketeer spends his time trying to encourage loyalty in his own customers and promiscuity in that of others. Consequently the result is that in many markets it is normal practice to lose half your customers from year to year. These changes do not happen overnight. They are the result of gradual shifts in beliefs and behaviour, which can go unnoticed, until it is too late.

Issues	Loyalty measures
• Encroachment on branded toothpaste by own label • Vulnerability of leading brands in context of growing consumer belief that 'all toothpastes are the same'	• In area of heaviest weight, growth of penetration in two years from 47% to 50% • Solus usage among users up from 31% to 40%

Action	Financial outcome
• Defence through attack • Drive of competitive advantage via explicit dental professional endorsement • Strong brand identity through graphics • Focus on empirical differentiation	• In the UK Colgate outperformed other branded toothpastes by 25% • Share up to highest level at 30% Colgate UK value share up 12% over two years. In rest of Europe, without corporate campaign, value share down 4% • Profit generated three times cost of advertising investment, in addition to strategic importance of maintaining strength as other brands declined in face of own label gains

Figure 11.6 Colgate: increasing loyalty in adverse circumstances

Issues

- Sales and share in decline
- Volkswagen perceived to be more expensive than it is
- Margin being given away by increasingly demoralised dealers because of need to convert higher proportion of relatively small prospect base
- Reduced overall profitability throughout business chain

Action

- Redeploy budgets from point-of-sale incentives to consumer communication
- Aim of increasing desirability of VW, thereby driving demand
- 'Suprisingly low prices' theme to enhance perception of affordability and value for money, regarding need to do deals

Loyalty measures

- Decline in proportion of attitudinally bargain-oriented, promiscuous prospects from 20% to 5% of buyers (those least likely to stay with a marque, the least profitable long-term customers)
- VW dealers themselves now showing highest level of satisfaction with own franchise of any in the industry

Financial outcome

- Fastest increase in sales of any brand of car in past 10 years
- % of buyers receiving no discount up from 10% to 27%
- Average 10% increase in actual price paid for each car relative to sector average
- Increase of dealer margin by 50%
- 10% growth in residual values and boost to second-hand market (historically the higher the retained value, the greater the intention to repurchase same marque)

Figure 11.7 Volkswagen: increasing profit by attracting a less promiscuous customer

Issues

- At time of launch, over 55 million 'loyalty' cards in circulation
- 74% of adults had one or more, with a quarter of holders owning 3+
- AGB data showing that the difference between owning and not owning a store card tended to be expressed in share of trips made, rather than higher spend
- Little apparent active use by companies of the captured databases, contrary to expectations

Action

- Focus of advertising strategy on positioning card as 'route to guilt-free indulgence', rather than as money-saving tool
- Link to Boots brand strategy of shifting positioning from medicinal to 'looking good, feeling good'

Loyalty measures

- Rate of card uptake double that of test area, where no advertising took place and the card was promoted in store via point of sale and prompting by assistant at time of purchase
- 33% of holders claimed that card ownership encouraged more frequent store visits
- 35% buying things they would normally have bought elsewhere (against 24% for their main supermarket card)

Financial outcome

- Only 29% claimed to use the card to get money off, against 68% for supermarket cards
- Spend increase of 9% on personal care items and 20% on cosmetics (focus of advertising, strategic drive areas for Boots and higher margin categories)
- Success of card highlighted in annual report as driver of business revival

Figure 11.8 Boots Advantage Card: using advertising to differentiate a loyalty tool

However, measuring loyalty goes beyond the simple analysis of buyer behaviour, which unless based on continuous panels, with their own attendant problems, can mask as much as they reveal.

Just as brands only exist in the minds of consumers, so true loyalty is an outcome of feelings as well as behaviour. This chapter contains three examples of research processes, which all recognise that loyalty and bonding need to be part of an holistic research process. Although the examples cited are all quantitatively based, they depend upon a close understanding of customer motivations, both at a category and brand level.

The role of advertising in generating loyalty tends to be diminished in much writing and the balance has shifted to communication areas which operate at a greater degree of customer closeness, typically loyalty cards.

However, if the principle is accepted that true loyalty is generated by building an *emotional*, rather than a *mechanical* relationship with a brand, then well-targeted advertising that is built upon a brand and consumer truth, is arguably the medium best placed to deliver this.

Further reading

Millward Brown International, *Brand Dynamics*, see www.millwardbrown.com

Reichheld, F., *The Loyalty Effect*, Harvard Business School Press, Cambridge, MA.

Taylor Nelson AGB, 'Grocery Retailing and the Loyalty Card', *Journal of the Market Research Society*, January 1998.

The NPD Group, *Brandbuilder*, see www.npd.com/corp/products/product_brandbbldr.htm

The argument in brief: Chapter 12

- Packaged-goods firms that put most of their marketing budget into advertising are more profitable (return on investment) than those that put most of their budget into trade and consumer promotions.
- Advertising works by helping to build strong brands.

Chapter 12

Long-term profitability: advertising versus sales promotion

Alex Biel

This chapter examines the allocation of funds between advertising and sales promotion. In recent years, marketers have been increasingly turning to sales promotion as a seemingly attractive strategy. Although many marketers agree that resource allocated to advertising is an investment in long-term brand building, there is far less confidence that advertising is an effective tool in the short or intermediate term. While it is generally accepted that promotions generate short-term sales, some of those sales are simply 'stolen' from future purchases by the same consumer.

There is a concern that this short-term orientation has destructive longer-term effects. A major question which marketers must confront is whether excessive emphasis on promotion actually erodes perceived brand value.

If a brand is on 'special' price too frequently, consumers are likely to start to think of the 'special' price as the normal price for the brand – and learn never to buy the brand unless it is discounted. Clearly, we need to pin down the benefits of sales promotion. Does it really build profits for a marketer, as conventional wisdom suggests? Or does it have a negative impact on earnings?

The long-term profit effects of sales promotion

Those questions led to the second collaborative study between the Center for Research & Development and SPI.[1] This time the SPI investigative team was headed by Robert D. Buzzell, Professor of Marketing at Harvard Business School. Again, the PIMS database was used.

For this second study, we further refined the database of 749 consumer businesses to examine businesses with basically similar promotional mechanisms. This led us to examine a group of 314 consumer non-durable businesses – the fast-moving consumer goods (fmcg) businesses included in PIMS, and on which we had both advertising and promotion spending data. Sales promotion, as defined in PIMS, includes both trade and consumer activities (the average US package goods marketer spends 60 per cent of his below-the-line money on trade promotions, and 40 per cent on consumer promotions); most consumer promotions relate to price: temporary cut-price offers, premiums, direct couponing and money-back deals. Contests, games and sweepstakes are also included in this category.

To examine the relationship between various strategies, on the one hand, and payout, on the other, the sample of business units was divided into three approximately equal parts, based on a frequency distribution of their allocation patterns:

- businesses using sales promotion as their dominant strategy
- businesses using a mixed strategy
- businesses using advertising as their major marketing investment vehicle.

Businesses using promotion as the dominant strategy were defined as all businesses spending less than 36 per cent of their marketing funds in advertising. The average business in this group spent only 23 per cent of their marketing money on advertising and 77 per cent on sales promotion.

The group using the 'mixed strategy' actually skewed slightly towards promotions. This segment of PIMS fmcg businesses spent between 36 per cent and 50 per cent of their marketing money on advertising. On average, they placed about 44 per cent of their marketing expenditures in advertising, and 56 per cent in promotions.

The final group comprised that set of businesses which used advertising as their dominant spending strategy. To be included in this group, businesses had to place over 50 per cent of marketing investment in advertising. The average business in this group allocated two-thirds of its marketing funds to media advertising, and the rest to promotion. Table 12.1 gives the performance of each group.

Table 12.1 Relationship of advertising/promotion mix to return on investment

Advertising/promotion mix	Average ROI (%)
Advertising emphasis	30.5
Mixed strategy	27.3
Promotion emphasis	18.1

Those companies spending the bulk of their funds – 76 per cent – on promotion, achieved an average return of 18.1 per cent (pre-tax and pre-interest charges).

Those employing the mixed strategy, where on average 44 per cent went to advertising and 56 per cent went to promotions, earned a considerably more respectable average return on investment of 27.3 per cent.

The group of marketers using advertising as their dominant strategy – that is, businesses investing more than 50 per cent of their marketing resources in advertising – registered the healthiest return on investments of all, averaging 30.5 per cent.

The other measures of performance included in the analysis, such as return on sales and share of market, all showed similar patterns; but as might be expected, the magnitude of the differences varied. It is clear that there is a positive relationship between the emphasis on investment in advertising and profitability. Conversely, those businesses that allocate most of their marketing budgets to promotion tend to have lower profit margins and rates of return on investment.

The effect of extra ad expenditure

One final piece of evidence comes from another source. These other data were developed by Information Resources Incorporated, a leading US research firm. They studied the impact of extra advertising spending on sales for 15 fmcg brands in a highly controlled experiment. The average brand they studied 'increased its advertising spending by 70 per cent during the one-year test.[2]

The IRI measurement system, 'BehaviorScan', is state-of-the-art, and quite high tech. It controls the advertising reaching test homes and measures what members of these households purchase through scanners at the checkout counters of stores in the market. This makes it possible to compare households receiving the extra advertising with a matched control group receiving only the normal advertising spend.

As Table 12.2 shows, the average increase in sales among those receiving the additional advertising pressure during the year of the test was 22 per cent. Not bad, but the story does not end there.

Table 12.2 Advertising-induced sales increase for
three years

Year	Average sales increase (%)
Test year	22
1st post-test year	17
2nd post-test year	6
Cumulative total	45

At the end of the one-year test, the extra advertising completely stopped. Both groups of households – the test group that had previously received the higher level of advertising, and the control group – received exactly the same level of advertising pressure over the next year for the test brands.

One year after the test, there continued to be higher sales among those households which had received the heavier advertising weight. These on average bought 17 per cent more than those receiving the base level advertising. In year three – two years after the heavy spending test – those who had received the higher weight during the test continued to purchase 6 per cent more of the average test brand than those in the control group. So it seems that additional advertising pressure has an enduring effect in addition to its immediate effect.

In another analysis of the profitability of more than 60 trade promotions using the same technology for data collection, IRI found that overall only 16 per cent of the promotions paid out. In addition, for established brands, the long-term effects were likely to be negative due to stockpiling by loyal buyers, on the one hand, and 'training' buyers to wait for deals, on the other.

Conclusions

The various PIMS and IRI studies lead to a series of conclusions.

First, when we look at advertising alone, it makes a measurable direct contribution to perceived quality, and share of market, which leads to profitability.

Second, advertising appears to have a carry-over sales effect that extends beyond the period during which it is actually running.

Third, when we separately examine the way in which businesses allocate their expenditures to sales promotion and to advertising, we see that those businesses emphasising advertising enjoy a higher return on invested capital.

Finally, we see a significant relationship between changes in market share and changes in advertising spending, but not between share changes and promotional changes. Clearly, money invested in advertising not only drives profits on a yearly basis, but also builds strong brands.

Design, packaging, public relations, sales promotion, experience with the brand and word-of-mouth all contribute to – or, in some cases, detract from

– these values. But advertising has traditionally played the leading role in shaping and defining the image of strong brands.

Evidence from PIMS shows that advertising makes a measurable, significant contribution to brand profitability. It does this in the year in which the advertising budget is spent, so there is an attractive *short-term* payout.

Data from IRI were also presented, however, illustrating that the carry-over effect of advertising continues to produce higher sales in the years immediately following the expenditure: a longer-term payout, and a welcome additional benefit.

Advertising produces these results by adding value to products and services. It produces these results by turning products and services into strong brands that have more leverage with middlemen; brands that can credibly pre-empt the truth; brands that enjoy higher loyalty; brands that are more forgiving of owners who occasionally stumble; brands that command better margins and are more resistant to price competition; brands that can be extended.

Advertising builds brands that mean more to the consumer. These brands can, in principle, live for ever. In other words, advertising works by building strong brands.

References

1. The Ogilvy Center for Research and Development, 'Advertising, sales promotion and the bottom line', 1989.
2. Abraham, M., 'Fact base design to improve advertising and promotion productivity', *Proceedings, 2nd Annual ARF Advertising and Promotion Workshop*, 1990.

The argument in brief: Chapter 13

- Four metaphors are proposed which dramatise the extraordinary power of advertising within the total communications mix:
    - *Advertising as DNA*: a code or imprint from which other communications inherit and learn behaviour.
    - *Advertising as glue*: sticking all the various parts of the communications mix together
    - *Advertising as a magnifying glass*: making other parts of the mix bigger and stronger and more effective
    - *Advertising as a megaphone or public address system*: a blast of encouragement which gets other parts of the mix going.
- However, in exploring how advertising can work in the total communications mix we are inevitably exploring the dominant or prevailing view of advertising: the paradigm. Looking back over the last fifteen years there have been two distinct phases in paradigm development.
- Today, we are entering a third paradigm phase in which advertising is beginning to show new self-belief. This follows a phase of confidence bordering on arrogance (late 1980s to mid-1990s) and then, after a crash in that confidence, a phase of self-doubt and crisis (mid-1990s to 2000).
- Advertising has changed as a result of this journey. It has emerged certainly more humble and possibly stronger. A key change from the past is the way advertising is now seen to play a number of important roles working *with* other parts of the communications mix, not working in isolation of them.
- Advertising is no longer in danger of extinction, as was predicted by some in the mid-1990s, because it is demonstrating how it can adapt and change.

Chapter 13

How advertising works in the total communications mix

Malcolm White

Looking back over the last fifteen years

I've just realised that my time working in advertising agencies now touches three decades: the 1980s (the late years), the 1990s, and now the first years of the new century.

Looking back over that time it seems to me that the dominant or prevailing view of advertising has changed. The broad preoccupations of the late 1980s have been replaced with different broad preoccupations, today. Who would have thought, back then, that the central role of advertising in the marketing mix would have been questioned, for example?

The changes in the prevailing views of advertising over this relatively short period have been manifested in the different propositions which new advertising agencies have launched, the revised mission statements of existing agencies, and the ways in which advertising has been written about by journalists and academics. Looking from the inside-out, these changes have also been characterised by changes in the language and jargon which people within the industry have used. As Charles Handy puts it 'words are the bugles of change'.

Between the late 1980s and the 1990s there have been two distinct phases. Each of these phases is characterised by a different paradigm. At the heart of each paradigm is a view of the role of advertising in brand-buildng; more central or more peripheral, and a perspective upon how advertising relates to the parts of the marketing and communication mixes. Each new paradigm has not invalidated the previous one, rather it has relegated it to a lesser position of importance.

Advertising had confidence bordering on arrogance in the period spanning the late 1980s and early 1990s. This was a boom time in terms of overall advertising spend, fuelled at least in part by the spend behind numerous privatisations. An equally telling, although smaller, sign of this confidence were the changes made to the pre-eminent IPA Advertising Effectiveness Awards in 1990. These changes encouraged case studies which could prove the longer and broader or brand-building effects of advertising, rather than just short-term sales effects. One might even say that during this phase there was an advertising-centric view of brand-building and even marketing. Advertising had a leadership role in relation to the other parts of the communications mix (if such a concept then existed?). Advertising was out on its own, literally 'above', the others 'below'.

During and following the recession of the early 1990s, advertising suffered from a declining share of total marketing budgets as more money was put into direct marketing, PR and other communications channels. Heinz's decision in 1995 to no longer use above-the-line advertising for brand-building but instead to use direct marketing to build relationships with customers was the *cause célèbre* of this shift. Even normally dispassionate commentators such as The Henley Centre became slightly hysterical: 'will mass-media advertising become the first dinosaur of the information age?'[1] they asked. As a response to these trends, many advertising agencies broadened their offering to include design, direct marketing and PR and to talk about through-the-line offerings and integration. The spirit of the time was captured by the brand consultant Judie Lannon writing in 1996:

> Advertising has dominated for decades..., but its dominance is now being questioned as companies look at their communications strategies in much broader ways. This requires the people planning such activities to address a different set of questions. First, the problem is no longer confined to 'How does advertising work?' If advertising is only part of the total communications plan, the next question must be 'How and why do all the other forms of communications work?'.[2]

Consequently there developed a more communications-centric view of brand building and marketing. Advertising's role became more chorus-line or cast-member rather than principal.

This was all difficult for advertising and people in advertising agencies but, as Judie Lannon implies above, the doubt and questioning around advertising certainly had some benefits in the longer term. As advertising was weakened so the other communications disciplines came out of this debate considerably strengthened. It was like a form of positive discrimination for communications.

In my view this was an extremely positive thing because it stopped at least some people in the advertising industry looking down their noses at other forms of communication. It encouraged some people in advertising to at least sometimes think outside the (TV) box, and it may have led to more effective communications campaigns as practitioners matched objectives to the right channels.

These two distinct phases are summarised in Figure 13.1.

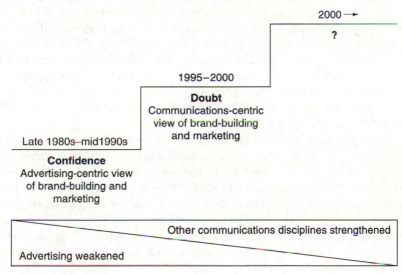

Figure 13.1 The two phases

The developments I have sketched out have affected the mindset and attitude of most of us in advertising. It has led to some of us in advertising agencies being too coy about the uniqueness and extraordinary power of advertising. A bit like women in the immediate aftermath of the impact of feminism who felt somehow to be letting their gender down to admit that they wanted to have kids and get married, so it was for some of us in advertising to say 'the ads are most important in this particular case' even when they manifestly were.

What is advertising's state of mind today?

As I said earlier, at the heart of the different advertising paradigms is a particular view of how advertising relates to the other parts of the communications mix. It seems to be the right time to consider the role of advertising in the communications mix because it feels as though we have recently emerged from a storm of self-doubt into a period of calm and reflection. The conditions for change are propitious. As the expert on scientific progress, Thomas Kuhn, put it when talking about the history of science:

> The emergence of new theories is generally preceded by a period of pronounced professional insecurity. Failure of existing rules is the prelude to the search for new ones.[3]

But those in advertising shouldn't be complacent and look forward to a new dawn of new theories, confidence and optimism. As recently as 2 May 2002, *Marketing* ran a double-page spread headlined 'Can brands grow without ads?' using the examples of Pizza Express, Pret à Manger, Dyson, The Body Shop and Marks & Spencer to show that advertising isn't always necessary to build strong brands. And, in the same article, according to the quoted IPA Bellwether report, above-the-line advertising accounts for only a slightly higher proportion of media spend (35 per cent) than Direct Marketing (26 per cent) and PR sponsorship (24 per cent).

But within that very article there are different views about advertising and specifically the role it plays in the communications mix. On the one hand, according to Mark Ritson, assistant professor of Marketing at the London Business School 'an ad campaign can steal the glory of a great brand launch'. On the other, in the same article, others talk about advertising in more positive terms. The IPA guide to what makes good and great advertising (*Shared Beliefs*) is quoted as saying 'a brand isn't a brand without advertising'. 'Brands tend to miss advertising when it's gone' says Dag Bennett, senior research associate at the Centre of Research in Marketing at South Bank University, and advertising holds everything together in the communications mix say others. Each of these different views suggests a different role for advertising and a different relationship between advertising and the communications mix.

Advertising's variety of possible roles in the communications mix

Close reading of the most recent of the case studies published in the IPA Effectiveness Awards and The Account Planning Groups Creative Planning Awards reveals advertising impacting upon the communications mix in a variety of different ways. Most of these different ways would not have been imagined in the late 1980s and I believe many of them would not have been possible had we not been through the period of doubt and insecurity characterised by the mid to late 1990s. They reveal advertising playing not one role but many, and advertising playing important roles *alongside* and *complementary* to other parts of the communications mix. Indeed, a key theme is how advertising is working hard to get the best out of the other parts of the mix. There is an echo here in current management thinking about leadership. Advertising in the new century is often the coach or mentor, not the dictator.

In order not to get bogged down in the specifics of individual cases, I've developed different metaphors which can illuminate the different roles and can function as general observations:

■ *Metaphor 1: Advertising as DNA*   Advertising can be a code or imprint from which other communications can inherit behaviour. Ads, especially brand-building TV ones, are dense with information and clues to who the brand is, what it is for, and who might wish to identify with it. Famous recent advertising campaigns for Tango, *The Economist*, Boddingtons, and Orange carry a particular DNA with them. And I don't mean executional equities such as endlines or characters, it is more subtle than this. Think of the relationship between Tango's infamous orange man relaunch TV advertising and the relaunch can designs. The ads will probably be familiar to you, but here is one of the can designs:

Figure 13.2 The Tango orange can. Reproduced with kind permission of Britvic Soft Drinks Limited

Now I don't know which came first, but I do know that they do not share any specific equities, just a strong sense of shared attitude or DNA. The way this relationship might work is alluded to by Paul Feldwick in a 1990 paper also following the IPA Awards, of that year. Referring to PG Tips, the Grand Prix winner of that year, he comments: 'It is clear that the advertising that played a major role in building the brand has become DIGESTED to become an inseparable part of it'.[4]

■ *Metaphor 2: Advertising as glue*   When specific equities are taken from advertising and used throughout the communications mix then the role of advertising is like glue sticking all potentially disparate elements together. There are lots of good recent examples of advertising playing this role: the AA's Fourth emergency service idea, the Army's 'Be the Best' call to action and the NSPCC's Full Stop campaign.

■ *Metaphor 3: Advertising as magnifying glass*   The highly awarded First Direct case study in the IPA Effectiveness Awards of 1998 (published in *Advertising Works 10*) shows advertising (in this case TV advertising) working hard to increase the effectiveness and efficiency of parallel media such as direct mail, press and posters. The TV advertising worked a bit like a magnifying glass making the other media bigger and strong and therefore more effective. The authors conclude their case as follows:

> Rather than belittle or discount parallel media, we are proud to have been able to build them in as an integral part of advertising's overall success, not obstacles or rivals to it. We are not claiming that television advertising is a panacea for all brand ills, but this paper should represent a strong exemplification of the extraordinary potential this 40-year-old medium still offers to advertisers.[5]

■ *Metaphor 4: Advertising as megaphone or public address system*   Advertising designed to get PR coverage feels like a pretty modern phenomenon. Here, advertising plays the role of a spectacular blast or noise which gets some of the other parts of the communications mix (especially PR and paid-for media such as newspapers) going. Very good examples of this would be the famous Eva Herzigova Wonderbra posters and political advertising of recent general elections.

These are only four significant and different ways in which advertising interacts with other aspects of the communications mix. The bigger point is that there is not one role but many. Advertising has extraordinary power but that power is today channelled in a greater variety of ways than it once was. The confidence bordering on arrogance of the late 1980s has been replaced by a self-belief tempered by humility won from struggle, doubt and questioning. Advertising as a discipline and a profession is better for it. Far from being an extinct dinosaur advertising is a good example of evolutionary behaviour. As Darwin put it: 'It is not the strongest of the species which survives but the one that is most adaptable to change.'[6]

References

1. The Henley Centre, *Planning for Social Change 1994/5*.
2. Lannon, J., 'Integrated communications from the consumer end part 1', *Admap*, February 1996.
3. Kuhn, T., *The Structure of Scientific Revolutions*, 1962.
4. Feldwick, P., *The Longer and Broader Effects of Advertising*, 1990.

5. Bryant, G. and Birkhead, B., 'First Direct – Advertising as a communications magnifier', *Advertising Works 10*, 1998.
6. Darwin, C., *The Origin of Species by Means of Natural Selection*, 1859.

The argument in brief: Chapter 14

- The effectiveness of an advertising campaign has always relied in part on the selection of the media channels used to deliver the message to the consumer. Implicit in this process of channel selection has been the assumption that the process is essentially one of maximising the exposure of the message for a given budget. This assumption stems from the military view of marketing: the consumer is a target to be aimed at, and with sufficient 'impacts' we can achieve the desired persuasion.
- This military model treats consumers as passive targets, yet in the modern media landscape they are anything but. With an abundant oversupply of media, increasingly controlled digitally, consumers now have an enormous degree of control over which messages they choose to receive.
- This chapter suggests a reversal of the traditional approach to planning media, which starts with the brand and looks for ways to push it into the consumer's head. Now consumers are in control, we have to start with them and ask ourselves why they would step forward to engage with the brand. In doing so we open up the campaign to a far wider range of media channels, from events to sponsorship, online to direct mail, and beyond.
- It's uncomfortable to accept that we are no longer in control of the communications process, but once we let go and accept that the consumer is in the driving seat then our thinking is no longer constrained by the traditional obsessions of media efficiency. The result is that we start to build campaigns around the people we are hoping to persuade. What starts by feeling like working back-to-front turns out to be the right solution for today's cluttered, commercialised world.

Chapter 14

How better media strategy leads to greater business success

Will Collin

Selling mints in Sheffield

Ever since I began my career in advertising I have wondered why this profession is felt to exert such a devious psychological influence on its intended target. If only this were true, I thought to myself, as I wrestled with my first challenge as a graduate trainee account planner: persuading C2D men to consume even more Trebor Extra Strong Mints. As I attentively sat in the corner listening to my boss moderating a qualitative discussion group in Sheffield, it was hard to see how any mere piece of advertising could manipulate these steadfastly down-to-earth people's day-to-day behaviour. They were quite plainly in full control of their relationship with the brand; a relationship that was rightly trivial, superficial and pretty much at the bottom of the list of priorities in their life.

Mints are not a big deal. It was obvious that the very best we could hope to do was to leave them with a half-remembered thought about the brand. This would hopefully be enough to raise Trebor a notch higher than other sweets in the lower reaches of their consciousness when they went to the paper shop to pick up a packet of fags. But it would never occupy more than a second's thought in and among their real preoccupations, be that the Wednesday game or their wife's birthday.

In the front room of a suburban house on the outskirts of Sheffield, it seemed clear to me from the start that the advertising we were planning to use to influence these men was indeed a feeble force in the wider context of their lives. Fortunately for us, even a feeble force could be enough to nudge them towards one brand over another when the decision between brands is not felt as being especially important. As my career progressed I came to learn that this view of the effect of advertising is called the 'Weak Theory'.

Yet the popular view of advertising is of mind-control and manipulation. If my knowledge of advertising history is accurate, this concept was originally popularised in the book *The Hidden Persuaders* by Vance Packard (Pocket Books of Canada, Montreal, 1957). This book 'exposed' the way that advertisers were now using subtle psychological techniques to manipulate people's desires; to get them to buy things they didn't need. Coming in an age of Cold War paranoia and a public fascination with the mysterious world of the subconscious as revealed through psychiatry, this conspiracy theory found a ready audience and has continued to exert an influence on the perception of advertising ever since.

> The use of mass psychoanalysis to guide campaigns of persuasion has become the basis of a multimillion-dollar industry. Professional persuaders have seized upon it in their groping for more effective ways to sell us their wares – whether products, ideas, attitudes, candidates, goals, or states of mind. (Vance Packard, *The Hidden Persuaders*)

As practitioners of the trade, we all know that advertising struggles to exert such a profound influence on people as that implied by Packard. If it did, we would find it considerably easier to persuade clients to invest their marketing budgets in this advertising rather than, say, in funding discounts and sales promotions. Of course it has an influence, but it operates at the margins of people's decision making and behaviour. This is often quite enough for the effect to be profitable, but it's a far cry from brainwashing a gullible public into unquestioning brand allegiance. (And mass psychoanalysis is one research methodology I have yet to encounter!)

My reason for this short trip down memory lane is to support my personal theory about advertising and indeed brand communication more generally: namely that we cannot, and have never been able to, 'target' consumers. They must choose to come to us, to participate willingly in the communication. If not, the message will not be received, no matter how heavy a campaign we wage against them. We cannot hoodwink them with subtle strategies; their inattentiveness and scepticism form a natural barrier against attempts to influence them covertly. Brand communication works when consumers want it to work. We cannot compel them to engage with us on our terms. Either we meet them on theirs or we don't meet them at all.

This is the basis for what could be called 'inverted marketing'. This means asking ourselves how we can enable the consumer to come to us, not how we can reach the consumer. It is the starting point for a new way of thinking about media strategy.

In an age of digital media, interactivity, fragmentation and consumer choice, the time has certainly come to reconsider the traditional marketing communications approach. While these technological developments have undoubtedly accelerated the phenomenon of 'consumer empowerment', I would argue that consumers have always been empowered. What I hope to show you is that accepting our impotence is the necessary first step towards adopting a much more powerful approach to planning communications.

This means war!

There is a long and distinguished history of using military metaphors to describe the process of marketing. We try to influence the 'target audience'. We do this by running a 'campaign'. We talk of deploying media like the British Expeditionary Force used artillery in Flanders: bursts, strafing, increasing the strike weight to deliver more impacts and thereby achieve greater penetration. The aim is to 'cut through', a phrase that suggests images of breaching barbed wire fences in no-man's land.

Just as military technology has advanced over the years, so the marketing metaphors have marched on in step. Now we often prefer a 'rifle not a shotgun' approach, using 'pinpoint targeting' like smart bombs in the Gulf War. And just as the modern military uses special forces to achieve objectives that conventional warfare cannot, modern marketing will sometimes deploy 'guerrilla tactics' when traditional techniques are ineffective.

These ideas have been the basis of several successful marketing books, such as *Marketing Warfare* (Al Ries and Jack Trout, McGraw-Hill Education, second edition, 1997) and *Guerrilla Marketing* (Jay Conrad Levinson, Houghton-Mifflin, 1986). For many marketing professionals, it seems, marketing does indeed mean war.

Because the language of marketing is the language of warfare, it is very difficult to think about brand communication in any other way. Yet if you think of communications in this way, you have to concede that the power balance is, and always has been, overwhelmingly in the consumer's favour. We are armed with pea-shooters, attempting to breach a massive citadel of consumer indifference. We can only succeed if they choose to raise the drawbridge and invite us in.

Consumers in the driving seat

Choice is the defining characteristic of the market economy. Nowhere is this more true than in the media, where the past 20 years have seen an explosion in consumer choice and a consequent fragmentation in consumption.

Arguably market forces came late to the UK media world; in the 1970s, when great consumer marketers like Heinz, Kellogg's and Cadbury's were already innovating like crazy to offer more choice, the media world was still heavily regulated and rationed as if it was still the 1950s. There was one commercial TV channel, only on-air for a limited time each day; an underdeveloped commercial radio sector; and a restrictive, slow-to-move press market.

That world is now long gone. Sky transformed TV by introducing multiple-channel choice, while VCRs and additional set ownership multiplied this choice further within each home. Union-busting and advances in print technology injected dynamism into the press, resulting in growth in newspaper sections and hundreds of new magazines. Commercial radio was progressively deregulated and has blossomed into the vibrant market it is today. And all this without mentioning the advent of digital media. This massive growth in media availability has created an enormous increase in consumer choice, and with choice comes control.

This control manifests itself in phenomena like zapping and zipping (fast-forwarding through ads on recorded videos). Or the way that many people 'multi-task' while consuming media, such as flicking through a newspaper while watching TV, or surfing the web with the radio on. In this world of media abundance, people are becoming adept at juggling and balancing their media consumption. The power to control what people watch, read and hear is moving away from the producers to the consumers. So much so that it is now often said that consumers are becoming their own editors and schedulers.

This is all quite apart from the control that has been ceded to consumers through the advent of new media technologies. Electronic programme guides (EPGs), near-video-on-demand movie channels and personal video recorders (e.g. TiVo) enable viewers to reach behind the broadcaster and get their hands on the TV schedule, so they can twist it into a shape that suits them. How long before we see third-generation mobile devices that act as radios, playing streaming audio off the Internet according to the listener's taste rather than the presenter's?

If it was true even before this explosion of media choice took place that successful brand communication relied on the willing complicity of the consumer, then it is doubly so today. Fragmentation and choice mean that we have to involve the consumer rather than just bombard them. If we persist in thinking about consumers as a target to be aimed at, then not only have they split up into smaller and smaller groups, but they are also armed with advanced defence technology to avoid our campaigns. Now, more than ever, we have to stop thinking warfare and start thinking participation.

Self-assembly brands

In recent times a number of marketing commentators have recognised that the shifting of power from producer to consumer is leading to a new way of thinking about branding. Instead of the brand experience being a fixed construct controlled by the marketer, the consumer gets to choose what kind of brand relationship they have.

In *The New Marketing Manifesto* (Texere, 1999), John Grant describes this process as follows:

> The trick with New Marketing is to relax a bit and let customers have their say, their part of the process. This is because we now have *A new culture of participation*. People expect to have a part to play and, when they don't, they feel shut out. The New Marketing response to this new culture is *Let customers participate as co-creators of the brand*.

(See Figure 14.1.) If this is true of branding then surely it must equally be true of communications. The consumer is in the driving seat. Successful communication results when they become involved: our job is to provide them with the elements of the brand message and then leave them to assemble the complete experience for themselves.

False gods

Inverted marketing runs counter to the traditions of media planning, which is based on the quest for cost-efficient delivery of a specific audience type. In traditional media planning the basic unit of communication is an 'impact': a

Figure 14.1 Old and new marketing. *Source: The New Marketing Manifesto* (Texere, 1999). © John Grant, reproduced by kind permission.

single exposure of the message to one individual in the target audience. Basing media strategy on the efficient delivery of impacts makes the tacit assumption that consumers are just passive recipients of the message; their minds merely empty vessels to be filled with brand imagery pumped in through media channels. Each impact delivered is like another drop of branding.

But in the brave new world of consumer control, 'impacts' are losing their impact. If the audience is indifferent, the supposed impact may be nothing more than a glancing blow, leaving little trace. This has always been true to an extent, because advertising is a weak force as the Trebor example showed, but with spiralling choice and control it has become a dangerous fallacy.

Yet the trading of media inventory, be that spots or space, is still based on the currency of the industry's syndicated research studies, whether BARB, NRS, RAJAR or whatever. These surveys audit the number of impacts that a given campaign will deliver, but shed no light on whether the message actually makes a connection when it impacts. So these studies play a critical role in underpinning the enormous market for buying and selling media, but are fundamentally based on the warfare school of marketing. It's like counting the number of letters delivered but without knowing how many of them have been opened and read.

Research studies that measure impacts offer false certainty. This seeming guarantee of communications effectiveness has created a veneer of accountability to certain media options that are measured in this way, while leaving others that lack the numbers seeming flimsy, fluffy or downright frivolous. Once you cast off the false religion of impacts, your eyes open to a much wider choice of communication options beyond those which traditional media industry research could quantify. This naturally leads to 'solution neutral' or integrated campaigns where the media selection is made-to-order, built around the consumer, rather than being drawn from the usual limited menu of standard options chosen for cost efficiency in delivering impacts.

To demonstrate how, the next section looks at two alternative approaches to a classic fmcg marketing challenge.

Inverted marketing: active participation, not passive exposure

The idea of inverted marketing is not to force your message on the consumer, but to invite the consumer to step up to engage with the brand's message on his or her own terms. One exciting consequence of thinking this way is that it immediately changes your perspective on which channels of communication might be appropriate. By way of demonstration, consider the following example.

You represent a detergent manufacturer which sells primarily to women with larger families, and whose brand identity is centred on caring for the family. You want to increase brand desirability among this audience to defend market share against cheaper competitors. What might your communications strategy be?

Following the marketing warfare approach you might create an ad campaign based on an empathetic, caring brand image. You would seek to maximise share of voice (i.e. out-gun the opposition) and if possible have a dominant advertising presence in the highest impact medium, TV. You might supplement your limited periods of exposure on TV with poster campaigns to build frequency of exposure, in order to build more of those crucial impacts.

But supposing we turn the problem on its head, and ask ourselves what we might need to do to encourage these women to step up and engage with us? We could start by looking at their daily lives. We soon discover the pressures they face, and the burdens of managing a family while holding down a job.

From this perspective, we might feel that TV and posters would offer a fairly shallow engagement with the brand for people who are in a constant state of juggling their limited time. Perhaps a better way to increase brand desirability would be by actually helping them. Maybe that would lead us to think about creating branded experiences that help them manage their family chores: for example, sponsoring a national network of homework clubs, creating a web database of approved childminders, mailing them cassettes of bedtime stories or GCSE revision guidebooks. The overall initiative might be spearheaded by a national survey, released to the press to coincide with the campaign launch, showing that British mums spend more hours working in one form or other than any other sector of the population.

Individually these ideas might feel like nice added-value extras, but collectively we begin to create an entire branded programme with which the audience will willingly engage, and far more deeply than with a conventional ad campaign.

This may sound like a fanciful idea: a consumer goods brand turning its back on mainstream media in favour of grass-roots activity. But that's exactly what Nike did with its successful 'Run London' amateur running event, or Tesco with its computers for schools initiative. It's true that they all need to use an element of conventional media to announce these initiatives in order to stimulate uptake, but ultimately the real connection they achieve is when the consumer steps up to connect with the brand, actively engaging with it.

How to plan an inverted marketing campaign

How should we respond to this shift in the balance of power towards the consumer? By changing the way we think about marketing communications.

Instead of pushing our message onto an indifferent public, we need to draw consumers in with relevant, timely and involving communications. In the old world of limited media supply it was enough just to have a great creative idea delivered to a (relatively) captive audience. A great advertising idea will still create a buzz, because people willingly get drawn into the message as they always have. But the bar has been raised for more run-of-the-mill executions that probably account for the majority of marketing campaigns. Now that the competition for our audience's attention has multiplied, the odds of our message making it through their filter are shorter than ever.

If inverted marketing is my recommendation for addressing this problem, what is the process for planning an inverted marketing campaign? The fundamental starting point is to understand the consumer well enough to be able to identify the circumstances where they might be willing to 'step forward' to engage with the message.

The following examples highlight several different opportunities for active engagement (and it's interesting to note that many of them are established advertising 'truths', which just goes to show that inverted marketing has been around a long time, without being identified as such).

1. Self-selection

When people enter the market for a particular product or service, their interest levels often rise dramatically, for example in insurance. Classically insurers build brand familiarity among a mass, uninterested audience using broadcast media and then use press advertising to communicate specific product messages to the narrow audience of those in the renewals market, who become temporarily sensitised to the ads that others ignore.

But when there is a self-selecting audience like this, it is a prime opportunity to capitalise on that interest with more than just a passive message. People will be willing to spend more time exploring the brand's offering because for that brief period the advertising has become actively useful to them. Long copy ads, decision trees, comparison tables and online product demonstrations all play to this state of mind. Perhaps this is the origin of the old direct marketing cliché, 'the more you tell, the more you sell', meaning that mailers containing more things to unfold and read tend to generate higher response rates.

2. Hands-on communication

When we talked 'involvement' in the world of traditional advertising we tended to mean the experience the consumer has when he or she becomes caught up in the narrative of the message, or held captive by the visual brilliance of the execution. But involvement can be taken more literally to mean their being actively involved in receiving the message. Either way this active process means the communication will be more memorable.

The challenge is to present the message in such a way as the consumer will be willing to take an active part in receiving it. A great example of this was an ad that ran in *The Guardian* to promote an article (the memoirs of Stella Rimington, former head of MI5) in an upcoming edition. In each copy of the paper there was a loose insert which appeared to be a piece of white card with a number of small holes cut in it. Printed at the bottom of the card was a message directing the reader to turn to page 3 of the newspaper and place the card over the poem printed there. On page 3 there appeared to be an obscure poem 'Of Love and War: Lost in Lille'. On placing the card over this there appeared a much simpler message: 'Stella Rimington former head of MI5 reveals all in the guardian this Saturday' (see Figure 14.2).

This idea effortlessly stimulates the reader's natural desire to uncover the hidden message, while at the same time rekindling a schoolboy fascination with codes and spying which would be a reason for reading the upcoming article. It is a great example of a message that the consumer has to take an active part in receiving – with enormous benefits for the brand.

This same principle applies to interactive advertising. I remember an excellent 'rich media' web ad for the *Financial Times* where I was able to pan around a stylish room containing a collection of objects all wrapped in pink pages, FT-style. As my mouse rolled over each wrapped object, for example a bottle of wine, I was informed how that topic was covered in the *Weekend FT*. Natural curiosity ensured I examined the entire contents of the room, and by the end I had learned that the FT at weekends covers a whole lot of lifestyle areas as well as the more usual business news. Once again, by encouraging active participation this ad gained greater attention and hence delivered its message more memorably.

3. Lifestyle support

Sponsorship used to mean paying for a brand name to be attached to an event, team, or programme in order that some of the positive values would become attached to the sponsor brand. But this is a rather passive approach, and too often the association appears superficial and unconvincing. However, when the brand moves from being a bystander to becoming the host, then its contribution is inextricably connected to the consumer's (hopefully positive) experience. For example, when Nike hosted the 10 000-metre fun run in London ('Nike 10k'), it was going beyond merely encouraging people to 'Just Do It' – it gave them a reason, devised a training plan, gave them regular reminders and created a desirable occasion to train for. This is an example of a brand's communication going beyond the passive delivery of a message and becoming 'lifestyle support' for its audience.

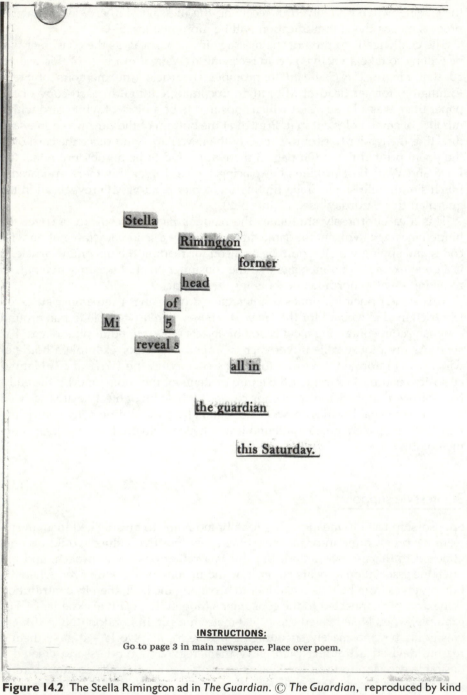

Figure 14.2 The Stella Rimington ad in *The Guardian*. © *The Guardian*, reproduced by kind permission. (a) The piece of white card with holes

OF LOVE AND WAR: LOST IN LILLE.

By Gustave Clemenceau (1919-1944)

Ah Stella! My Love and Sorrow!
Down in the Rimington's garden
We kissed goodbye my former pain
I stroke your head, your gentle hair
Was made of gold – and then I left:
Milan, for 5 long weeks,
I can reveal so much
Then back to France, all in love for you
And you were gone.
You were gone, the guardian of your house
Said so.
But I'm going to battle this Saturday.
Will I see you again? *Je ne sais pas.*

Translation by Nick Lucas

Figure 14.2 *(continued)* (b) The complete poem

Another great example of 'lifestyle support', coincidentally for one of Nike's main rivals, is the street sports event 'Reebok Sofa Games', held first in Dublin and then in various mainland UK cities. Rather than just running a TV commercial (excellent though that was: the man trying desperately to escape the demon sofa that tried to prevent him from leaving his flat to go running), Reebok recognised the need to bring consumers closer to the brand through active participation. They created a live event into which consumers were drawn through a combination of traditional poster ads, radio sponsorship, 'e-flyers' virally distributed on e-mail, and even second-hand sofas branded with the event's web address and strategically placed on street corners. The *pièce de résistance* was a motorised sofa driven through the streets to be captured on film for the benefit of the press (Figure 14.3).

Consumers were drawn into the event by a process of discovery, which is far more powerful than simply being passive targets. Once at the event, people were able to take part in a range of activities, from skateboarding to live DJs to 5-a-side football that created a much deeper connection with the brand than could have been achieved just through a conventional ad. The end result was a

Figure 14.3 The Reebok Sofa Games marketing activity. Courtesy of Reebok International Ltd, reproduced by kind permission

demonstrable improvement in brand desirability which saw Reebok leapfrogging its nearest rival.

4. Usable messages

Advertising doesn't always have to struggle to gain people's attention: sometimes they find it actively useful. Classifieds are the obvious example of this: messages that are actively sought out to answer a specific need for information.

In a similar manner, in the financial services market consumers often use the personal finance press as a tool to aid their decision making. They scan the ads in newspapers as well as the editorial, using both as sources of information, taking from them what they need. The role for advertising is not to persuade them in a single hit that a particular product is right, but to present them with useful 'factoids' which they can incorporate into their decision along with other influences such as friends' advice and information from leaflets and branch staff. Even when people consult a financial adviser they will often 'arm themselves' with a little information from advertising so as not to appear completely ignorant.

Similarly, in the marketing of new film releases, advertising is known to be a very weak influence alongside word of mouth and reviews. Nevertheless consumers use advertising to provide updates about new releases, and as a guide to times and venues. Advertising helps fuel the 'talkability' surrounding a new release, but it's unlikely to persuade someone to see a new film by itself.

By recognising how consumers use advertising in particular circumstances, the opportunity exists to set out deliberately to harness this behaviour. Intelligent Finance, the e-finance subsidiary of Halifax, took a regular advertising site alongside the best-buy tables in the newspapers' personal finance sections. Recognising that their primary market would be financially hands-on people who conduct their own research, IF helped them do what they would have done anyway – compare its rates with the competition. By making it easier for them it increased its chances of being included within the consideration set in the first place.

Summary

Advertising is not a sophisticated form of mind control enslaving helpless people into buying things they don't need. Quite the opposite: it is a weak force, usually operating at the margins of people's decision making. It is the consumers who are and always have been in control, either through a simple lack of interest or more recently because the abundance and controllability of modern media gives them this power.

Yet so much of the theory of marketing treats consumers like a target to be hit, not people to be persuaded. The vernacular of marketing is the language of warfare. This mindset encourages us unthinkingly to consider the role of media to be one of accurate and efficient bombing – hardly conducive to engaging people as individuals. The 'target audience' becomes a distant mass of bodies to aim at, not a group of people to be understood, seduced and converted. And with increasing consumer sophistication as well as media fragmentation, the battle to reach them gets harder by the day.

We are looking at consumers the wrong way. Instead of starting with the brand and trying to work out how to push it through to the consumer, we need to start with the consumer and ask ourselves why they would want to connect with the brand. This is the basis for inverted marketing: asking ourselves how the brand should offer up its message so that the consumer will come forward to engage with it, rather than trying to plan ever more efficient ways to push our message onto an indifferent public.

This way of thinking leads to a range of ideas for encouraging consumers to become actively involved in brand communication, where we harness people's natural characteristics – such as curiosity, self-interest and scepticism – so that the messages are willingly embraced. The alternative is to work against the grain, trying to squeeze the brand communication through people's ever-narrowing filter of inattentiveness.

I have called this process Inverted Marketing because it starts 'the wrong way round'. But in a world where consumers are in control, it's becoming the only sensible way for building effective communication.

The argument in brief: Chapter 15

- This chapter examines the concept of what is 'effective advertising'.
- It argues that there are some key lessons to be learnt from recent IPA award-winning papers.
- It highlights the benefits of:
  - Joined-up thinking
  - Diverse approaches to evaluation
  - Recognising advertising's unique power
  - Integrated creative ideas.

Chapter 15

Tangible demonstrations of the advertising contribution

Chris Baker

The case histories which emerged as Award or Special Prize winners represent excellence in one or more of the following criteria: the sheer scale of the effect achieved; originality in thinking and/or execution; telling us something new about how advertising works; overcoming an intrinsically difficult advertising or evaluation task.

The winning entries represent a widely drawn sample of 'effective advertising' – and indeed successful brand marketing – in recent times. They provide a unique 'window' on the state of the art in advertising and its evaluation, and brand marketing generally.

The individual cases will repay detailed inspection. But, in addition, some overall observations emerge.

'Joined-up thinking'

Although not their primary objective, these cases provide insight into the processes associated with successful advertising and what it is that advertising agencies do for their money. This could be characterised as 'joined-up thinking' across several stages: *Information, Analysis, Understanding, Insight, Ideas, Advertisements, Media implementation, Exploitation* (e.g. PR, promotions, distribution leverage), *Evaluation,* and *Resulting next steps.*

Case histories are inevitably somewhat simplified, sanitised and revisionist in their treatment of what actually happened. 'Insider experience' of the process suggests that it would be wrong to regard the above as discrete, and so potentially 'unbundlable', stages. Rather they tend to blur one into another, with multiple feedback loops. The separation of creation from strategy neglects the fact that strategy is often informed by creation. The separation of evaluation from subsequent strategic thinking can also result in a loss of quality and sensitivity. Jeremy Bullmore, described this way of working – which he regards as central to the value agencies add to their clients' businesses – in a recent speech:

> In real life, as we well know, it's a seemingly endless and circuitous sequence of gathering knowledge, generating hypotheses, finding an expression for them, getting reactions to them, interpreting rather than accepting those reactions, modifying, rejecting, starting again, inviting intuition, guesswork, luck, regrouping, re-introducing discipline, checking again against real people.
>
> Scientists lie about this process at least as disgracefully as advertising people because it doesn't sound either scientific or manly. In fact, of course, it's both. Those of us with a fondness for long words know this way of working to be called hypothetico-deductive; but it's almost never overtly apparent in the advertising it inspires – any more than a sound knowledge of anatomy will be overtly apparent in a good life drawing.[1]

The Boddingtons case history is an excellent example of both the process and value of 'joined-up thinking'. Boddingtons had three marketing objectives which could easily point in three very different directions: the creation of a major national take-home brand; the creation of a major national pub brand; the protection of its regional heartland. To realise these objectives so completely with, in effect, a single campaign is no mean feat – it required considerable strategic and creative insight, and a *holistic* view of the overall task. It is difficult to see how the Boddingtons solution could have been achieved without a multi-skilled team of people working very closely together. Of course, this does not necessarily mean that all these people have to work for the same company, but the 'advertising agency concept' certainly provides an environment where these kinds of results are more likely to happen.

Peperami is another argument against 'unbundling'. From the outside, success could be put down to just a stroke of creative brilliance. The case history makes it clear that there was much more to it than that. Insights from semiotic analysis and 'confessional interviews' with users put the Creatives into the right area. Creative input to strategic development research then helped to refine strategy. Subsequent pre-testing gave the client confidence to run the very bold work that went on to produce such dramatic results in the marketplace. Media planning – which led to the advertisements developed being placed into programming where they would most stand out (as well as effectively reaching their target audience) – was also a key factor. This helped to deliver advertising awareness – which in this case was the main driver of sales – that was the highest in the broader 'snack' market with, in competitive terms, a relatively limited budget of £800 000.

Diversity and evaluation

The winning cases remind us that advertising can play different roles, which mean timescales for success can also be very different. Cases such as Peperami and Boddingtons relate to dynamic change and rapid payback as a result of advertising. For others such as BMW, British Airways, and Cadbury's Roses a longer-term perspective makes the power of advertising most vividly apparent. The AIDS case history perhaps puts this into sharpest relief – early and continued commitment to communicating about this issue has much to do with the UK being a 'low AIDS prevalence' country (compared to other European countries which chose 'not to talk about it').

If any further evidence is required to undermine the value of simplistic, standardised uni-dimensional approaches to advertising research, then the reader will find it from inspection of these case histories. They remind us that successful advertising can work in a number of ways – in Terry Prue's terms, *persuasion*, *involvement* or *salience*, or indeed across two or even all three of these models. Each of these models can be 'supercharged' by exceptionally high advertising awareness or retarded by low advertising awareness.

The Award winners also show diversity in terms of ease of measurement. In some cases the contribution of advertising can be measured relatively easily and immediately.

But in others (the majority), demonstration of the commercial impact of advertising is considerably harder, particularly in the short term. This is inconvenient but unsurprising. Increasingly marketing success is driven by factors which conspire to make the evaluation of advertising more difficult: high levels of *integration* and resulting interaction across the mix, making it harder to isolate what's doing what; *consistent* relationship building (albeit frequently refreshed by innovation or other 'new news'), which is harder to measure in the short term than variability; *new thinking* which challenges the conventional roles of the game, rendering established norms less useful.

Nevertheless, many of the cases show that 'hard to measure' doesn't mean 'can't measure'. Most use some form of 'argument by elimination': i.e. they examine the overall performance of the brand over time (sales and profitability); dispose or otherwise take account of all potential influential factors both 'internal' to the brand and contextual (e.g. price, distribution, weather). Advertising effects can then be inferred from the residual, with 'corroborative' evidence provided by consumer research measures such as awareness, image and usage. The accumulated weight of evidence can produce a solid, but still ultimately circumstantial, measure of advertising effectiveness.

This of course begs the question of the 'base level assumption' – *what would have happened without advertising?* Any evaluation needs to understand the underlying trend of the brand, which is rarely simply to stand still. The 1992 Milk Marketing Board case history[2] was based on reducing the rate of sales decline rather than sales growth. The Arthur's catfood case history is similarly based on the maintenance of equilibrium via advertising in a situation where competitive factors were against the brand. Making realistic 'base level of assumptions' often means looking *outside* the brand to develop external competitive benchmarks. The BMW, British Airways and AIDS case histories were particularly good examples of this, comparing their performance with that of close competitors (BMW, British Airways) and/or the same 'product' in different countries (BMW, AIDS).

'Only advertising can do this'

In a world of multiplying marketing and communications possibilities – and increasing 'cohabitation' of advertising with other marketing techniques within integrated campaigns – it is easy to overlook advertising's unique properties, and the fact that other marketing techniques are rarely a true alternative to it. Advertising can of course often be justified simply in 'cost per thousand' terms (i.e. the cost of delivering the desired message to a given audience), but its real uniqueness stems from two related factors: (i) its power to grab people's attention, excite their interest and capture their imagination and (ii) its ability to create an atmosphere in which other elements of the mix become more effective, and it simply becomes easier to do business. The Award Winners put advertising's unique properties in high relief. Here are four of the most striking examples where it would be hard to disagree that 'only advertising can do this':

1 BMWs are excellent and innovative cars. In the car market *the car itself* – allied to value for money – is the most potent element of the marketing mix. Despite being relatively expensive in the UK, BMW's long-term sales and image growth in the UK greatly outstripped its performance in other European markets where it has not enjoyed the same quality and consistency of advertising support.
2 The Wonderbra is a highly individual product which had been on sale in the UK for 26 years. In early 1994 its new owner, Playtex, faced the threat of a me-too competitor launched by the old licensee, Gossard (the Ultrabra). Despite this, sales have

almost doubled, due to a cleverly deployed £330 000 advertising spend which has generated directly related PR with a notional value of £18 million.

3 In the 1980s British Airways had the image of a 'run of the mill' nationalised industry. Since then its fortunes have been transformed, in terms of both profitability and perception. The product has been re-engineered, but research shows that competitive service standards have improved too. If British Airways had not shouted their ambition to become 'The World's Favourite Airline' loud and wide would customers have noticed the change, and would staff have responded to deliver it?

4 Boddingtons' draughtflow device was a wonderful idea – at last bitter drinkers could get the same experience at home as in the pub. But Boddingtons also sell cans without the 'widget' and these have increased their sales as well. And pub sales have increased dramatically too, well above that which can be explained by distribution gains.

Innovation, creativity and brands

The evidence of these awards run counter to the pessimism in some quarters about the future of brands and advertising. But it also confirms that ever more competitive market conditions set more exacting standards for brand and advertising success – in particular, a greater commitment to innovation, creativity and continuing to offer your customers real value. It is those who lack commitment to this more dynamic concept of the brand that tend to fall by the wayside.

With the benefit of hindsight, in the hedonistic 1980s the concept of 'adding value' via advertising and other marketing action often lost touch with reality. David Hearn, of KP, once observed, 'adding value' had become synonymous with sticking gold stripes on your packaging and charging more for your product.

In the last 12 years, it was perhaps not surprising that a high proportion of the most successful advertising appears to be founded more on the communication of *integral values*, rather than simply 'added values'. Advertising based on the communication of *fundamental product truths* – albeit in a very creative way – has come much more to the fore.

These 'product truths' may be based upon product innovation and ongoing product improvement – BMW, British Airways, Boddingtons, and John Smith's Bitter are exemplars of this. Alternatively they may come from extracting the full value from existing, but under-exploited, appeals of highly individual products: for instance, Peperami, Wonderbra and Marston's Pedigree.

This is not to suggest that the 'added' emotional values which differentiate powerful brands from good products are any less important. Rather it is to say that success tends to be even more dependent than previously on these 'added values' being associated with a good and innovative product, and ideally strongly *integrated* with (not just attached to) this product.

Despite this refocusing on product truths, creative advertising remains very much an integral part of brand innovation, not just a messenger of it. Indeed, despite being judged on the criterion of commercial effectiveness, a high degree of creativity is a consistent ingredient in the winning entries. They highlight among other things something that smart advertisers have long known: that 'creative' advertising does not just add value, *it saves you money*. Successes such as Peperami, Wonderbra, and the Nissan Micra come from advertising spends which, in a broader competitive context, are relatively low.

The high level of creativity witnessed in the most recent Awards continues a long-term trend observable since 1980. For most of the 1980s the majority of winning cases were characterised by well-planned strategies, and 'on strategy' but fairly average advertisements. The more sophisticated and challenging conditions of the 1990s tended to demand rather more for success in the marketplace: not just well-planned strategies and 'efficient' execution, but also a high degree of creativity.

'Effective creativity' has come to mean much more than just creative *advertisements*. It embraces creative thinking on a broader front about strategy, the use of media and other ways in which a product or service can be communicated to its target market.

References

1. Bullmore, J., 'Advertising costs half as much as you think it does: but do you know which half?' published by the IPA, December 1994.
2. Baker, E., *Advertising Works 7*, NTC Publications, 1992.

PART D

Brand Effects

The argument in brief: Chapter 16

- Product and brands are not the same thing. There are many fewer brands, and fewer still successful brands.
- Brands are more than products. They are products plus extra values, products plus communications in all its forms.
- Brands are much more complex than products and are about much more than functional performance.
- Brand success is determined by the extent of 'motivating differentiation' in relation to the competition.
- Advertising's contribution is to present the brand totality in as compelling a way as possible, to generate brand preference.
- It is particularly able to harness (and convey) a brand's 'heart appeal' to its more functional attributes, an ability increasingly important for brands in a world growing ever more complex and competitive.

Chapter 16

The advertising contribution to brand preference

John Bartle

Introduction

Advertising stands or falls by its contribution to better business performance. (Better, that is, than would have been the case without it – and to a level which, over time, justifies its cost.)

It can make this contribution in a number of ways against a variety of target audiences. It can make short-term announcements – a sale, a promotion, the latest prices, a new store opening. It can be used almost as PR against opinion leaders. It can help to boost a share price or City standing. It can be used to encourage a positive 'trade' response – better shelf space, more prominent presentation. It can help to instil pride, confidence and 'appropriate behaviour' into a company's employees. It can simply provide information, as much government advertising does, for example.

Advertising is nothing if not versatile. But primarily, its particular contribution is in helping to build and sustain brands, developing and maintaining preferences which, over long periods of time, provide the bedrock of successful consumer businesses.

To fully understand the nature of this contribution we need, most of all, to understand brands; what they are and how they are constructed.

Products and brands

Products and brands are very different things. (Here and hereafter the word 'product' is used to include services as well as just physical entities.) While there are very many products there are relatively few brands, and fewer still that could lay claim to being successful – or on the way to being so – and, thus, truly being part of that company 'bedrock' just mentioned.

There is still nothing that better illustrates the product/brand difference than that most basic of market research: the product test. When tested, by consumers, in a 'blind' product test – i.e. with the brand identity completely masked – you will get one result. With identity revealed, with 'branding' added, you will get another, different one.

There is some, though little, published evidence of this fundamental phenomenon. In Figure 16.1 two products are tested against each other, identity unknown, and also, among another perfectly matched sample of the population, with identities revealed. A parity in taste preference in a 'blind test' becomes a clear preference for one (Brand B) when the two products are named.

In a second example (Table 16.1), where the brands being tested are named for the reader as well as for the research respondents, there is a turn-around in preference without and then with disclosure.

(It is important to appreciate that, in both examples, these results are from questions on product performance – taste preference – whether presented blind or identified. They are not buying intention or brand preference responses though that, of course, is precisely what they reflect. Consumers in these tests *are* saying that the products taste differently when they know which brand each product actually is.)

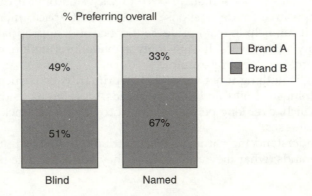

% Preferring overall

Figure 16.1 Blind versus named product test. (*Source:* King[1])

Table 16.1 Blind versus named
product test: diet colas (%)

	Blind	Branded
Prefer Diet Pepsi	51	23
Prefer Diet Coke	44	65
Equal/don't know	5	12

Source: de Chernatony and Knox[2]

From product to brand

What is clear – from these examples and all one's experience – is that pure product performance can and will be altered when all aspects of identity are brought to bear, when consumers bring their preconceptions, prior experience and beliefs to the actual usage experience. Things can taste better, perform better, or worse, either absolutely or, crucially in our competitive world, in relative terms.

This change will always take place. The examples quoted illustrate the rule not some exceptions to it. If, in a true branded market, you find no change from blind to branded response then that will be coincidental and an exception. (In 'quasi product tests' in service industries where identical service offerings are presented, though attributed to different service providers, exactly the same phenomenon will be evidenced; some seen as much more appropriate than others.)

None of this should be taken to suggest that basic product performance (the 'blind test' bit) is unimportant when building a strong brand. It should be a fundamental part, but only a part. Only a part because brands are much more than their basic product offering; they are products with extra values. The extra values are communications in all its forms.

In real life products do not arrive naked but 'clothed' as far as consumers and potential consumers are concerned. There will be some very direct, immediate clothing – the brand name itself, identification of the company behind the brand perhaps, a pack design, the packaging format, its pricing and, very importantly, one's own prior experience of the brand, if any. Less direct but also part of this clothing will be what one has heard about the brand from other people, users or not, from what you read and from what you see, whether provided and paid for by the manufacturer or not.

All of this, mixed individually by each person, will determine brand choice and brand preference, whether this is a brand 'for me'. Will this brand deliver for you (and yours) in your eyes – a judgement which may also include how others will view you as a result of that choice?

From a whole host of factors, therefore, comes how a brand is perceived, comes what is real to consumers, comes what he or she is actually faced with in determining brand preference. While the basic product offering is part of the brand, the brand is much more besides.

The complexity of brands

Brands are much more complex, multi-layered and multi-faceted than products. They are much more than the functional performance.

Figure 16.2, derived by combining several different sources, attempts to illustrate the totality of the brand. (To the original sources the word 'delivery' has been added to remind us all that, without a satisfactory delivery against consumer expectations, no brand, however skilfully constructed, can be complete, strong or successful over time.)

Figure 16.2 illustrates the two broad areas, the rational and the emotional – 'head' and 'heart' – which combine to make up any brand. On the one side are the functional attributes – as measured in these 'blind' product tests – on the other all the communication elements which surround the basic offering. It is when these two broad areas are *taken together* that the total brand picture is produced (and those branded product test results).

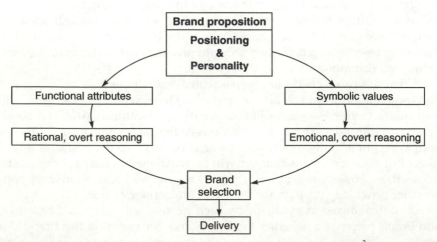
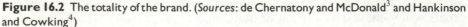

Figure 16.2 The totality of the brand. (*Sources:* de Chernatony and McDonald[3] and Hankinson and Cowking[4])

Brand success

Brands are products with extra values attached. No extra values, no brand. So, while every brand has a product or service within it, not every product can lay claim to being a brand.

These extra values are in many cases 'intangible' values; they are feelings, images, associations, the statement something makes about you to others. They are not to be taken lightly or invented with no reference to consumers. Rather they are to be valued and respected since they are fundamental to our nature as social human beings.

The communications industry talks often of 'added value' in this context as synonymous with these extra values, but this is too loose a usage. A moment's thought – and reference to our earlier product tests – will suggest that brands can have extra values that subtract value, most certainly so in relative terms, in the competitive context where real life takes place. (And we will all have our examples of when the extra values actually undermine the product in absolute terms too.)

The extent to which extra values are genuinely 'added', in the consumer's eyes, will be the key determinant of a brand's relative strength and success. This will determine the degree of differentiation of a brand from its competitors.

The absolute key to brand success is *motivating differentiation*. Differentiation which creates what Stephen King has described as 'a bit of a monopoly in the mind of the consumer'. Only from this can the value of the brand be fully derived.

Truly successful brands, as well as providing consumers with a believable 'guarantee' via their identity, also provide a *mélange* of values – physical, aesthetic, rational and emotional – that is seen by consumers as, in combination, particularly appropriate, thus worth seeking out, worth paying for and with the perceived promise met (or exceeded), worth paying for again. On such brand success is business success built.

The advertising contribution

In its brand-building role, the major contribution that advertising can make is in its ability to communicate the brand totality talked about earlier, the crucial combination of the rational and emotional, the 'head appeal' and the 'heart appeal'. In particular, advertising can add emotional values in a way that no other marketing element can. Its multi-facetedness and its potential subtlety mean that it can appeal to the senses and affect the emotions in a way nothing else can with the same permanence, not least because we live in such a visually literate age with increasingly marketing-sophisticated consumers.

And, in a world of increasing complexity, the ability to add the emotional, more intangible values (the right-hand 'leg' of Figure 16.2) is becoming more and more important. The crucial requirement of differentiation is less and less readily delivered on the functional level. Competitors are smarter and faster than ever. Technical leads can disappear almost overnight.

The days of the USP (unique selling proposition) built on functional superiority are very largely gone, certainly in any enduring sense. Increasingly this needs replacing by what we might call the ESP (emotional selling proposition) to deliver sustained brand success.

This is not to argue that the functional is of no importance. It is important in combination with 'heart appeal' and all the strongest brand propositions are rooted in a product truth, even if that truth is not unique. Emotional appeal alone will result in emptiness, will stay superficial and will be found wanting in time. Increasingly, though, it is what is added on the emotional side that creates its uniqueness, its differentiation, its 'bit of monopoly' and, therefore its success.

This area is pre-eminently the province of advertising. This is where and how advertising makes its contribution to brand preference.

References:

1. King, S., *What is a Brand?* J Walter Thompson, 1971.
2. de Chernatony, L. and Knox, S., 'How an appreciation of consumer behaviour can help in product testing', *Journal of the Market Research Society*, 32, 1990.
3. de Chernatony, L. and McDonald, M., *Creating Powerful Brands*, Butterworth-Heinemann, Oxford, 1992.
4. Hankinson, G. and Cowking, P., 'What do you really mean by a brand?' *Journal of Brand Management*, August, Henry Stewart Publications, 1995.

The argument in brief: Chapter 17

Currently, there is a range of different tools available to marketers to help inform their understanding of the process by which activities such as advertising produce returns. Many are useful in isolation but, it is only when they are applied together and, most importantly, from the perspective of the economic value they are generating, that they can begin to produce a truly complete and actionable picture.

Econometrics tends to be directed at the effects of specific elements of the marketing process. Brand Valuation and Brand Equity are more macroscopic in nature. Brand Valuation captures the direct economic benefit of the brand to its owner in its current use while Brand Equity looks at its current state and potential relative to the market, competitors and stakeholder groups. All are critical to understanding the value chain. Hence, although synergy has become an overused and somewhat ill-defined word recently, these three present the opportunity for a true synergy in this context as the interactions between them will result in a much greater understanding than separately.

While it is this greater understanding that is the key to assessing 'return on investment' (ROI), turning it into a simple calculation is invariably confused by the complexity of defining the investment and the time period in which it delivers. To do this, it is useful to think of return on investment in terms of the incremental effect on brand value. This is after all, by any sensible estimate, the bottom line as far as the brand and therefore for any tool designed to work through or leverage it, is concerned. Given that, we can then conclude as to both the value of the brand per se and the extent to which investments to build or leverage it delivers shareholder value.

Chapter 17

How advertising affects brand value

Simon Cole

Introduction

As the Brand Economy gathers momentum, so too does the belief in the need to understand the extent to which investment in brands generates returns. CEOs of most businesses now recognise the importance of brands – at least if their comments in press releases, annual reports and analyst's presentations are anything to go by. The danger remains, as with similar blandishments about employees and human capital, that the link between investment in brands and the financial results of a business remains opaque, little studied and insufficiently understood.

Clearly, the importance of a brand as a business asset needs to be intelligible if it is to command an appropriate share of resources. The efficiency of mechanisms such as advertising, by which a brand converts investment into profit, needs to be clear. If the means by which brand levers such as these work are transparent they can then be organised to best effect. For that to happen there has to be a more complete answer than is currently the case to the disarmingly simple question, 'how does brand investment generally and marketing or advertising communications in particular create value and deliver economic return?'

Over the last 50 years much work has been done to understand marketing communications in all their forms. More recently a considerable body of research has been directed at brands and their 'equity'. Furthermore, there are many academic and business publications that consider how companies create value and how to value them; indeed, each of these specialisms supports an entire industry. Notwithstanding that, it remains the case that although these three elements of the value chain are often well understood individually, they are considerably less well understood collectively, i.e. in how the value chain connects and functions as a whole.

In order to address this shortcoming and start to join the different parts of the 'knowledge bank' together, brand owners are increasingly trying to orchestrate the overall management of their brands and take direction from the economic value they represent. Such an approach, founded on the principle of brand valuation as pioneered by Interbrand in the late 1980s, takes advantage of recent developments that have established clearer links between each step in the path to value forged by brand support tools such as advertising. Thus, it has become possible to not only begin to answer the question as to the extent to which say, advertising is turned into economic profit, but more usefully, how, why and indeed what might be done to improve it.

Brands as the foundation of economic value

The cornerstone of any assessment of marketing communications must always come back to the 'brand'. The brand is the sum of all thoughts, feelings and impressions of the product or service to which it is attached and is by definition located in stakeholders' – e.g. consumers' – heads. Advertising and marketing communications are processed in those consumers' heads where they guide, accelerate or reinforce any thoughts and impressions, invariably doing so in conjunction with all other 'brand messages' emanating, for example, from personal experience or perhaps competitive comparisons.

By that argument, communication tools should be thought of as either (or both) building or leveraging the brand to encourage choice over an alternative, ultimately, in order to produce profitable consumption. Consequently they should be judged accordingly. Assessments that relate volumes or share of expenditure to sales or brand share, whilst sometimes useful, tend to be so overly simplistic that while attractive on the surface, are in truth contributing little to the understanding of how, how much or arguably most importantly, how profitable, any returns are.

The brand is the basis on which customer demand is generated and secured. Advertising, and marketing more generally, adds to or leverages the 'power' of the brand in the shape of a stronger brand equity which, when 'filtered' through external constraints such as accessibility produce incremental sales, the first step to enhanced economic value. The brand is the mechanism through which advertising and marketing communications produce economic value (ultimately shareholder value in public companies), and as such, presents the logical basis from which to measure their contributions (see Figure 17.1).

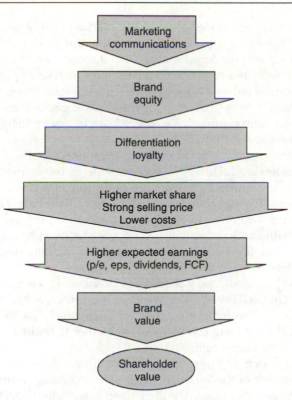

Figure 17.1 Marketing communications ultimately produce shareholder value

From micro to macro measurement – the need for holistic assessment

Over the years much has been written about the process by which marketing communications such as advertising work. Many different points of view and theories have been expressed and many arguments waged. Invariably, the only point of general agreement is that the value chain is invariably complex. In all that, what has not been adequately addressed is that the different elements work in concert and so need to be assessed as such.

Many different tools have been developed to provide insight into individual parts of the value chain. While these can often produce a level of detailed understanding of one particular aspect, their scope is almost always limited. Damaging consequences can then result if that skewed 'understanding' is applied to a brand's communications strategy. For instance, 'effects' may be overstated because of an implicit assumption that the contribution 'identified' is a consequence solely of the marketing tool under examination. In that case, 'minor' inputs such as less impactful media or other drivers of brand equity are underestimated in favour of 'dominant' inputs. Alternatively, with many different advertising, marketing and brand levers working in some kind of harmony albeit in different ways, effects are often divided in such a way that any potential synergistic consequence of their interaction goes unrecognised, i.e. the whole is erroneously assumed to be the sum of the separate parts.

Clearly there are a number of different components whose contributions all need to be understood. However, this must be in recognition of the fact that they may be operating as a consequence of, or in conjunction with, each other.

The challenge facing brand managers is how to take a view of the value chain in its entirety in order to understand the contributions of the components both individually and collectively. With such a perspective they can more effectively control the range of marketing tools at their disposal to greatest short and indeed long-term benefit.

Seeking such a holistic view should not be viewed as attempting to produce some 'Grand Unified Theory' of marketing, but rather, as taking the best of the tools available and reconfiguring them in such a way as to orchestrate their application and have them complement each other to build a 'complete' picture in order to enable better control.

The value of such an approach is considerable. Above all it will produce a realistic assessment of the 'end benefit', i.e. the economic return on investment. More importantly, perhaps, it will deliver a sufficient level of insight and understanding of a complete value chain to enable the development of practical and sensitive mechanisms to manage the application of spend, media and messaging to best effect.

Configuring the route to value

In order to develop realistic and actionable insight into the benefit of marketing activities such as advertising, it is first of all necessary to have a clear understanding of the location and drivers of the brand's economic value. Then, in conjunction with an assessment of the brand's equity and the immediate impact of the different communication tools (i.e. on to and leveraging specific elements of the equity) it is possible to derive a sensitive model of total value production (see Figure 17.2).

In the light of this 'complete' understanding the overall return on investment can be accurately identified and, most importantly, be used, *ceteris paribus*, to inform future communications and brand strategy.

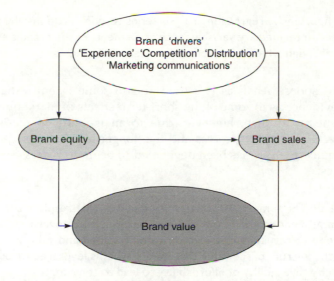

Figure 17.2 A model of total value production

Populating the value chain model

A number of tools are available to populate this model. Each one can inform an individual specific part of the value chain. Together, they become more powerful and start to reveal a much deeper insight and begin to explain value delivery overall.

- *Marketing Response Analysis*: Econometrics, or more likely, regression analysis has been used with considerable success in recent years to isolate and quantify some of the effects of marketing activities. On the surface it would appear to offer a powerful means to link marketing (or indeed any other input) to 'hard indicators' such as sales. As a result its contribution to understanding how marketing adds value has been considerable. It must also be noted however, that the possibilities it presents have sometimes been overestimated:
  - While it offers a useful means to identify some of the short-term effects of marketing activities its ability to distinguish longer-term effects is questionable.
  - While it can provide good evidence of 'effect' when inputs are varying, when they are constant or moving in parallel, their impact is much more difficult to see and therefore often missed.
  - While it tends to offer a quick and easy view of customer demand its ability to sensitively disentangle the inevitably complex combination of drivers of purchase is limited.

– Most importantly, regression analysis tends to offer little insight into the all-important intermediary variables such as elements of the brand's equity or the factors through which it is leveraged to create demand.

Marketing Response Analysis is a tried and to some extent tested means of providing evidence as to some of the short-term effects of marketing activity. It is insufficient on its own, however, due to an inability to model both the 'internal mechanics' of the process and the 'longer-term' effects.

Brand Equity analysis has been developed to begin to redress some of these shortcomings.

■ *Brand Equity*: The sum of all distinguishing qualities that result in and dictate personal commitment to the brand. It is the qualities that govern preference for a brand over an alternative that lead to it being valued and valuable. The brand's equity is the fulcrum of the value chain and is what is leveraged through external factors such as availability or affordability to lead to consumption.

Brand Equity, by definition, resides in customers' (or any stakeholders') heads and must consequently be assessed in that context to be properly understood. The most effective approach to this involves three steps.

– Primary consumer research data to capture the current marketplace state of the brand.
– Analysis to identify first, those factors that are influencing consumer commitment or likelihood to consume and second, the extent of that influence. This is the identification of the overall 'power' of the brand along with its principal drivers and associated elasticities (Figure 17.3).

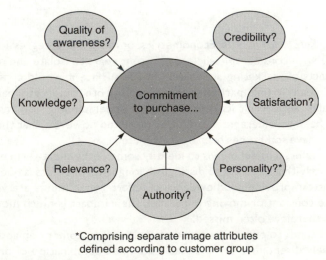

*Comprising separate image attributes
defined according to customer group

Figure 17.3 The overall 'power' of the brand

– Target customer segmentation to identify Brand Equity by customer group in the competitive context.

The insight produced from a detailed understanding of the brand's equity provides a thorough understanding of customer behaviour. In that, it is a powerful complement to the insight produced by Marketing Response Analysis. To complete the link, however, the learning produced by both tools must be tied back to the economic reality – the brand's value.

■ *Brand Value*: Brand Value represents the economic benefit delivered to the owner or user of the brand delivered by its current use. It is the sum of the current and expected earnings (discounted to a net present value) attributable to the brand.

  Brand Value is created at the point of transaction and is determined by three factors. First, the extent to which the brand owner can generate economic profit from that transaction. Second, the degree to which the brand is instrumental in the transaction, i.e. in driving customer choice. Third, the likelihood that the brand will continue to exert its influence in the future. A calculation of Brand Value is therefore made up of three steps:

  – Financial analysis: To yield a profit and loss forecast adjusted to approximate to free cash flow over time; a charge to remunerate the tangible capital is made leaving the residual earnings attributable to the intangible assets operating in the business.
  – Demand analysis: To determine the importance and Role of Branding; by applying the Role of Branding percentage to intangible earnings, the earnings attributable to the brand can be identified.
  – Brand Risk analysis: To assess the Brand Strength and thus security of the brand franchise from which an appropriate discount rate is derived to calculate the Net Present Value of expected brand earnings – the value of the brand (see Figure 17.4).

Calculating the return on brand investment

Having completed the three phases of analysis described above it is only a short step to identify 'return on brand investment' or, for example, 'return on advertising investment'. Moreover, having populated the entire Value Chain model it can be applied both 'backwards' – to assess the economic contribution or effectiveness of earlier investments – and forward – to model the likely value impact of different investment scenarios. In that, brand owners are equipped to understand not only the payback of alternative options but, more usefully, how those investments could best be made – in terms of scale, media and message – to have the greatest likelihood of success.

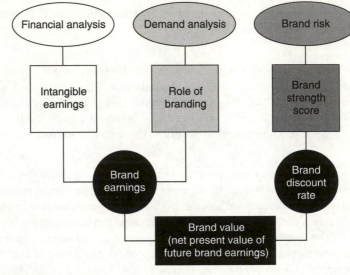

Figure 17.4 The Brand Value

Understanding the payback of marketing tools such as advertising by this means recognises, and captures the incremental economic value manifesting at the different stages of the value chain. Moreover, it is only through such a holistic approach to value creation that a complete picture of how much 'return' (and why) can be painted. One that is sensitive to impact in the three main channels of the brand value model namely:

- Revenue growth: through the objective assessment of the short-term 'result'
- Greater 'brand influence': through the objective assessment of the increased contribution of the brand to customer demand
- Increased brand strength: Through the objective assessment of increases in the likelihood of the brand to secure future demand.

Conclusions

The advertising and marketing processes under examination are understandably complex and as a result the only way to understand them with any certainty is to bite the bullet and take a holistic view such as described.

Doing so will undoubtedly be more costly in time, resource and financial investment but it is necessary and indeed ultimately more cost efficient if the brand owners are to manage their brands as effectively as they must and so compete successfully. Indeed, given the levels of expenditure on advertising and branding generally and the relative scale of the economic asset companies have tied up in brands, it is arguable that such an approach is rapidly moving from luxury to necessity.

The argument in brief: Chapter 18

- Typically, and as is to be expected, within a product category there is a positive and significant relationship between the size of a brand in sales terms and the size of its advertising expenditure.
- A larger brand has more resources, and therefore in absolute terms is very likely to spend more on advertising than a smaller brand. This is why we compare **share of voice** with **share of market**.
- For example, all other things being equal, it would not be surprising to find that the share of advertising spend (SoV) for a brand with a 5 per cent market share (SoM) was half that for a brand in the same market with a 10 per cent SoM. But of course in practice, all things are rarely, if ever, equal.
- In the practical world, the relationship between SoV and SoM in a market is not uniform, and the purpose of this study is to examine whether changes in this relationship are systematically connected with subsequent sales changes.

Chapter 18

Advertising and the long-term success of the premium brand*

Stephan Buck

Share of Voice versus Share of Market: earlier work

The seminal database in this area was established by Jones[1-4] and usefully described and adapted by Broadbent.[5] In 1987, advertising and brand share data were collected across many countries for a total of 1096 brands. Jones first broke these down into two groups:

- **Investment Brands** (overspenders) – where SoV was greater than SoM
- **Profit-taking Brands** (underspenders) – where SoV was less than SoM

The study found a tendency for small brands to have proportionately larger SoVs than large brands, i.e. there were a greater proportion of investment brands among the smaller brands. This can partly be due to the fact that for larger brands, advertising works harder, i.e. there are economies of scale. But the relationship can come about because new (small) brands usually require advertising investments that exceed their initial market share, while some older and often larger brands are 'milked' in order to provide short-term savings and

*Adapted from Buck, Stephan (2001) *Advertising and the Long-term Success of the Premium Brand*, published for the Advertising Association Economics Committee by WARC.

higher profits. Table 18.1 provides one of the important results of the 1987 study.

The correlation is by no means perfect (e.g. even 41 per cent of the larger brands are investment brands) but the very large sample base has apparently revealed a basic relationship. It follows from these results that the difference between SoV and SoM tends to be higher for smaller brands. This led to the development by Jones of the AIC (advertising-intensiveness curve) which was tabulated on the results of 666 brands in packaged goods markets (see Table 18.2). This relationship has been used as a budgetary planning tool.

Again, study of Table 18.2 shows that the relationship is not a perfect one. For example, despite the fact that in the table the **average** difference (SoV − SoM) for the 13–15 per cent SoM group is **positive** (value of +1), results from Table 18.1 show that more than 50 per cent of brands in that group have a SoV **less** than their SoM. Given the variability that therefore exists between brands within a share group, for all the practical reasons described above, it seems doubtful that these average findings would be very helpful in deciding the effects of changes in adspend for a specific brand. In other words we have reservations about the use of these average findings for operational purposes[*] although the general relationship is an interesting one.

Much of the early work seems to concentrate on the absolute differences between SoV and SoM and how this is related to brand share. It would seem both intuitively and mathematically more sensible and desirable to work with the ratio SoV/SoM rather than the absolute difference. First, SoV/SoM for a brand is equivalent to its advertising to sales ratio relative to its competitors in

Table 18.1 Smaller brands spend proportionately more on advertising

Share of market (SOM)	% Investment brands (SoV > SoM)
1% to 3%	73%
4% to 6%	63%
7% to 9%	59%
10% to 12%	55%
13% to 15%	44%
16% and over	41%
All brands	56%

Source: Jones[2]

---

[*]As Broadbent points out in a general context,[5] ... 'I don't manage an average brand, so why should I rely on the average?'

Table 18.2 The advertising intensiveness relationship

Share of market (SOM)	SoV-SoM (percentage points)
1% to 3%	+5
4% to 6%	+4
7% to 9%	+2
10% to 12%	+4
13% to 15%	+1
16% to 18%	+2
19% to 21%	0
22% to 24%	−3
25% to 27%	−5
28% to 30%	−5

Source: Jones[2]

the product category and therefore has particular meaning. Second, whilst an absolute difference of say 3 percentage points of SoV is the same in absolute cost terms regardless of brand share, it surely would be expected to have more relative effect on a brand with a 3 per cent market share than on a brand with a 30 per cent market share.[*]

SoV versus SoM for the current study: comparison with earlier work

The association between SoV and SoM can be made for 1975, the base year of our study, and then for the more recent years. A number of caveats need to be made in relation to comparison with earlier work:

1 Our study concerns the number 1 and number 2 brands within 26 different fmcg categories. As such, the brands tend to be relatively large (average of 26 per cent brand share in 1975). The distribution of brand shares is positively skewed compared to previous studies.
2 With a maximum of 52 observations, the variability that exists due to other factors in the marketplace (described above) might mask any basic relationships that exist.
3 Retailers' Private Label in the UK is significantly higher than in most other countries. Private label is not generally advertised, and therefore it follows that the average SoV will be higher than the average SoM, where the latter is measured on the total market category. It follows that, on average, SoV−SoM will be positive and SoV/SoM >1.

---

[*]To quote Barwise[6], '...everything is relative to the competition. What really matters is relative Adspend (as a proportion of sales, the advertising/sales ratio)...'

This was pointed out by Jones[1,2] but not taken into account in his subsequent analyses. The effects may not have been very marked in 1987 when private label was less significant. Also, Jones was dealing with results from a multi-country study including territories where private label does not figure highly. The effects are likely to be more relevant in our study, since not only is private label very prominent in the UK, but it has increased significantly from some 16 per cent in 1975 to 29 per cent in 1999 for the 26 markets in this study. This point is investigated further below.

Of course, the imbalance between SoV and SoM, due to the presence of private label and other non-advertised brands, needs to be taken into account in the UK in particular when setting advertising budgets. An obvious solution is to compute market shares on the base of advertised brands only.

4 The Jones study used volume data in calculating market shares, whilst our data uses expenditure. Again, this may affect the average levels but should not alter the basic relationships to a great extent.

For all these reasons, it would not be surprising if some of the results of this study turn out to be different from those of the Jones study. However, if there is a real and significant connection between SoV and SoM, it should show up in our work, and our first task was to examine this at a high level of generality.

Figure 18.1 gives the scatter diagram comparing SoV with SoM for 1975, the initial year of the study; results for the other years where both SoM and SoV are available are very similar. Generally, and as expected, higher market shares are associated with higher shares of voice although, given the particular conditions of certain markets, the relationship is by no means perfect (correlation of 0.75).

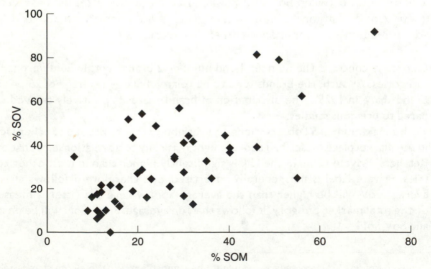

Figure 18.1 Scatter diagram comparing SoV with SoM for 1975

Table 18.3 SoV and SoM averages for brands grouped by size (1975 and 1999)

	1975		1999	
	Brands <22% share	*Brands >22% share*	*Brands <23% share*	*Brands >23% share*
Average SoV minus SoM	+5.8	+4.4	+9.9	+12.5
Average SoV/SoM	1.5	1.1	1.6	1.3
% Investment brands	57%	57%	61%	74%

Source: Taylor Nelson Sofres plc

Table 18.3 compares the average levels of SoM and SoV for the brands grouped by size; results are presented separately for 1975, the initial year of this study and for 1999, the final year. The columns showing the average differences between SoV and SoM and the ratio of SoV to SoM allow an opportunity of comparison with the original Jones results described above, albeit on a much smaller database.

Before drawing comparisons with earlier work, we need to take into account our earlier caveat, which draws attention to the significant role played by retailers private label products in the UK. For this reason and because some other brands in the marketplace do not advertise, the values of average SoV must necessarily be greater than average SoM, where we have calculated the latter across all brands in the category.

To illustrate the effect of this, Table 18.3 is repeated, but removing from each product category the private label proportion of the market share (Table 18.4).

Table 18.4 SoV and SoM averages for brands grouped by size (excluding private label share)

	1975		1999	
	Brands <28% share	*Brands >28% share*	*Brands <23% share*	*Brands >23% share*
Average SoV minus SOM	+2.4	−2.5	+4.3	−2.5
Average SoV/SoM	1.2	0.9	1.1	1.0
% Investment brands	43%	43%	55%	42%

Source: Taylor Nelson Sofres plc

The elimination of private label increases the market share of the remaining brands, and therefore alters the dividing line between large and small. When analysed in this way, the results are closer to those in the Jones study. The SoV of smaller brands is greater relative to SoM than larger brands in both 1975 and 1999. There was no difference in the share of investment brands in 1975, but by 1999, smaller brands showed a higher propensity to invest.

Brand success related to share of voice: some previous results

One of the important results of the original Jones study was a measure of the extent to which brands with a rising share were investment brands (SoV > SoM). His results for larger brands (above 13 per cent market share) show that 48 per cent of brands with 'a slightly rising share' were investment brands compared to only 37 per cent of brands that were on a 'slightly falling share'. Furthermore, a Jones analysis confined to larger brands in packaged goods markets showed that brands with a rising sales trend were on average more likely to have a higher SoV relative to their SoM than brands with static sales. Brands with a declining sales trend had, on average, lower SoVs in relation to their SoMs than static brands.

This suggests that the maintenance of a relatively high advertising to sales ratio plays a part in the subsequent success of a brand. However, the segmentation of brands into 'rising' or 'falling' groups was presumably accomplished from a knowledge of recent sales trends leading up to the period on which the analysis was based. This will mean that it was difficult to separate cause and effect (as Jones makes clear) in the sense that success in the marketplace might lead to larger advertising budgets and thus to higher relative SoV.

The data available to us in this current study allows us to move in the other direction, i.e. we can measure the extent to which a relatively high SoV in the base year is correlated with a brand's subsequent success.

Brand success and share of voice: some new results

Earlier research has quantified the fact that many individual brands that were number 1 or number 2 in their product category in 1975 had continued to prosper over the years, so that in 1999 they occupied similar positions or had even strengthened those positions. And this despite the significant inroads made in nearly all markets by retailers' private label products over the years. Not surprisingly there were other brands that fared less well and some that did very badly. In some cases, the losing brands were a victim of changing tastes, rationalisations or acquisitions, but we need to investigate the extent to which broad advertising expenditure played a role. We can segment brands based on their progress over the years 1975 to 1999 into three groups:

1 **Group 1 (Losers):** Brands losing rank position and share
2 **Group 2 (Static):** Brands maintaining rank position but losing share
3 **Group 3 (Winners):** Brands maintaining rank position and gaining share

Table 18.5 looks at the initial 1975 relationships for each group between their share of voice and their share of market.

It is clear that the brands that did well over the years tended to have a higher relative advertising to sales ratio than the less successful brands. An analysis of variance shows that the differences between the three groups approaches significance ($p = 0.11$), while the difference between the 'winners' and the other two groups is significant ($p = 0.036$).

The success or failure of a brand over a 24-year time scale will obviously depend on many more factors than the advertising to sales ratio in the base year. To investigate the association over a shorter, more recent, period, an analysis was carried out of the extent to which brand share trends over the period 1995 to 1999 were associated with relative advertising to sales ratios in 1995 (see Table 18.6).

The sample sizes are small (each has about nine brands) but the pattern of results seems clearly to point to an association between the progress of a brand and the degree to which its share of voice exceeds its market share ($p = 0.07$).

Table 18.7 provides corresponding results for the periods from 1995 to 1997 and from 1997 to 1999 respectively; both data sets illustrate again the relationship that growing brands tend to have relatively higher advertising to sales ratios.

It must be emphasised that our criterion for brand success is growth in market share, not profit which is virtually impossible to separate out for a single brand, normally part of a large conglomerate. There is not always a link between growth in market share and in profits – the former can be bought in the short term at the expense of the latter. However, such disequilibrium rarely lasts long. Loss-making dashes for growth are not a recipe for continued

Table 18.5 SoV relative to SoM in 1975 for three brand groups

Brand groups based on performance from 1975 to 1999	Average SoV – SoM 1975	Average SoV/SoM 1975
Losers	1.6	1.0
Static	2.1	1.2
Winners	11.1	1.6

Source: Taylor Nelson Sofres plc

Table 18.6 SoV v SoM related to brand share trends (1995 to 1999)

Brands grouped by SoM changes 1995 to 1999	Average SoV — SoM 1995	Average SoV/SoM 1995
Falling by 2 or more share points	−1.5	1.1
Falling by up to 2 share points	−0.3	1.0
Rising by up to 2 share points	+11.4	1.6
Rising by 2 or more share points	+21.8	1.9

Source: Taylor Nelson Sofres plc

Table 18.7 SoV v SoM related to brand share trends

	Performance 1995 to 1997		Performance 1997 to 1999	
	Average SoV — SoM 1995	Average SoV/SoM 1995	Average SoV — SoM 1997	Average SoV/SoM 1997
Falling static brands	3.5	1.2	4.7	1.0
Rising brands	10.5	1.4	14.4	2.0

Source: Taylor Nelson Sofres plc

brand survival: the longevity of successful brands suggests that growth in market share is an acceptable proxy for brand success. If this is the case, it seems undeniable that there is a relationship between maintaining a high share of voice and creating a brand that will remain successful over a long time period.

References

1. Jones, J. P. (1989) *Does it Pay to Advertise.* Lexington Books.
2. Jones, J. P. (1992). *How Much is Enough?* Maxwell MacMillan International.
3. Jones, J. P. (ed.) (1999). *How to Use Advertising to Build Strong Brands.* Sage Publications.
4. Jones, J. P. (ed.) (1999). *The Advertising Business.* Sage Publications.
5. Broadbent, S. (1989). *The Advertising Budget.* NTC Publications Ltd.
6. Barwise, T. (ed.) (1999). *Advertising in a Recession.* London Business School/ NTC Publications.

Taylor Nelson Sofres superpanel data is the copyright of Taylor Nelson Sofres plc.

The argument in brief: Chapter 19

In summary, advertising and marketing communications can help the corporate brand to achieve more in terms of its relationships with all its stakeholders, and thus business success, than if it were to rely just on personal contact and word-of-mouth reputation.

There is a clear causal link between higher awareness, or 'fame', for a corporate brand and more favourability towards it. Sheer 'likeability' in its advertising and marketing communications aids corporate awareness, thus completing a virtuous circle for the brand.

Among many things, strong corporate brands can:

■ Create competitive advantage in the battle to attract and retain customers
■ Add leverage to the relationship with suppliers
■ Improve investor relations
■ Help attract and retain good employees
■ Enhance the perceptions of the management and company among opinion-formers in the governmental, financial and journalistic worlds
■ Add leverage in mergers and acquisitions
■ Improve relationships within the local communities in which it operates.

Chapter 19

How advertising works for corporate brands

Hamish Pringle

Corporate versus consumer brands

The understanding of the power of branding and its application to products and services has spread far beyond the traditional consumer-goods marketers who invented the discipline. It used to be the case that 'corporations' were rarely considered to be brands, because they sold to other businesses rather than individual customers.

When the likes of ICI embarked on their corporate advertising campaigns in the late 1960s and early 1970s they were very much in the minority. Nowadays for corporations in almost every industry, their branding is important in a way it never was before.

The concept of the 'corporate brand' has moved from one concerned with shadowy, behind-the-scenes holding companies to a multiplicity of organisations which must have a high profile as a key part of their make-up, even if their actual business-to-business customer base is numerically small.

Transparency and the interactive era

One major factor in this is the advent of the era of 'transparency' brought about by the increasingly ubiquitous and intrusive media, and of course the Internet.

This has been driven in part by the democratisation of shareholding, which has made so much more corporate news of personal interest to millions outside the core financial community where it originally used to be contained.

Transparency has also been enforced by the increasingly vociferous consumerist lobbies, which embrace a spectrum of issues that are challenging to the corporate world and demand a response: environmental pollution, sustainable development and Third World labour to name but three. Rare is the company that does not have a website, a call centre or a helpline. Citizens with a complaint can access a wealth of company information with a click of their mouse, request a response by e-mail or simply phone the CEO's office. This is why it's increasingly important for the corporate brand to align its internal values with its external ones, and so ensure a seamless and holistic response to customers.

Corporate brands in the global economy

The Internet also enables business-to-business customers to access a vast range of potential suppliers. In this potentially bewildering environment, strong brands act as signposts for buyers in a market that's crowded to the point of being overwhelming. As the global economy develops, enabled by ever more sophisticated supply chain management and driven by economies of scale, corporations need to reach customers in markets geographically distant from their home base. A strong corporate brand acts as an ambassador when companies enter new markets or offer new products. It also shapes corporate strategy, helping to define which initiatives fit within the brand concept and which do not.

That's why companies which once calculated their value strictly in terms of tangible assets have increasingly realised that a strong brand is an equally important if intangible one, which must be nurtured and protected too. The stockbrokers of the world now realise that a strong corporate brand has the power to command a premium price among customers, and support that company's share price in the markets. Hence the growing interest in brand valuation.

Four main types of brand architecture

There are four main sorts of corporate brands, which operate along a spectrum. This stretches from one end, where the corporation stands behind operating companies that themselves offer a range of different products or services under individual and distinctive brands, to the other end where the company is itself the brand. Schematic 'brand architectures' for the four main types are described below.

First, there is the scenario (see Figure 19.1) where the corporation is the umbrella organisation, often a publicly quoted plc, beneath which usually unlisted subsidiary companies operate, which in turn market brands to customers.

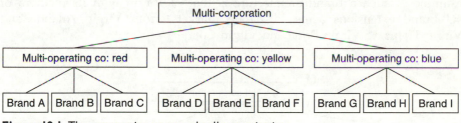

Figure 19.1 The corporation as an umbrella organisation

An example of such a brand architecture is Unilever, which owns a series of company brands like Lever Fabergé, Unilever Best Foods and Birds Eye Walls, each of which in turn markets a range of strong brands with individual identities such as Persil, Hellmanns and Magnum.

One of the attractions of this structure is the high degree of insulation between the front-line brands and the quoted holding corporation two levels above it. In some instances companies, which have suffered from negative publicity concerning one of their operating companies of the same name, have changed the holding company identity to create some 'distance' between them. Woolworth changing to Kingfisher and Saatchi & Saatchi to Cordiant, and back again, are examples of this strategy.

Second, there is the architecture (see Figure 19.2) where the company markets a series of product or service brands, under separate identities and names, which bear no relation to the company itself, but where its name or logo is used as a 'house' endorsement. This is the situation with Pfizer with its Benylin, Sudafed and Viagra brands.

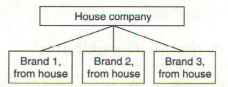

Figure 19.2 The company markets a series of unrelated products or brands

Usually these 'house' names are featured in a subsidiary manner on packaging and in advertising, with the main brand identity to the fore. The cumulative effect of billions of exposures adds up to a valuable reputation for quality, assuming of course that the individual brand performance is good. Thus the house name becomes a brand in its own right and can be a very effective endorsement, especially in assisting the launch of new products.

Third, there is the case where the corporation is effectively the brand (see Figure 19.3) and sells a product range, which is essentially marketed under the same identity, but with sub-brands used to distinguish particular lines. An example of such a brand architecture is that of Virgin with its plethora of sub-brand extensions across disparate markets, from Virgin Atlantic and Virgin Trains, to Virgin Bride and Virgin Cola.

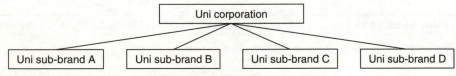

Figure 19.3 The corporation is effectively the brand

Fourth, there is the instance (see Figure 19.4) where the corporation *is* the brand and where it is hard to discern much more than generic descriptors for the products or services it provides to its customers. This is true in the case of retailers such as Pizza Express or Gap, single-product companies like Rolls-Royce or Orange, multinationals such as BP or BT, or even media owners such as *The Sunday Times* or MTV.

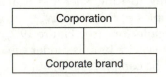

Figure 19.4 The corporation *is* the brand

The common denominator of 'fame'

What all these corporate brands have in common, and indeed share with many product brands, is that sheer awareness is closely correlated with favourable perceptions. (Of course being infamous for poor product or service performance or the neglect of corporate citizenship can be damaging too.)

This fundamental idea that the first step towards building a customer relationship is simple awareness was brilliantly encapsulated by the famous McGraw-Hill advertisement reproduced in Figure 19.5.

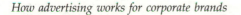

"*I don't know who you are.*
I don't know your company.
I don't know your company's product.
I don't know what your company stands for.
I don't know your company's customers.
I don't know your company's record.
I don't know your company's reputation.
Now—what was it you wanted to sell me?"

MORAL: Sales start **before** your salesman calls—with business publication advertising.

McGRAW-HILL MAGAZINES
BUSINESS • PROFESSIONAL • TECHNICAL

Figure 19.5 Simple awareness. © The McGraw-Hill Companies, Inc. Reproduced with permission of The McGraw-Hill Companies

Between familiarity and likeability

Thus advertising and marketing communications can influence corporate brands very positively just by raising the pure level of awareness and familiarity. Familiarity easily translates into favourability or likeability, the most powerful component in a brand's reputation. Hard evidence that familiarity and favourability have a close and positive correlation is provided by the long-standing MORI tracking research study of corporate reputation. This can be seen clearly demonstrated in Figure 19.6.

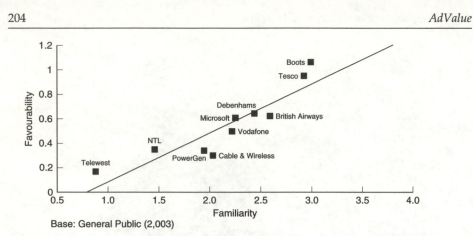

Base: General Public (2,003)

Figure 19.6 The MORI study of corporate reputation. (*Source*: MORI, November 2000)

McGraw-Hill's advertising proposition that a higher spontaneous brand awareness translates into a greater propensity to do business in reality is confirmed by data from the financial services industry provided by Ipsos-RSL in Figure 19.7.

At its most basic, the corporate brand must ensure that, through advertising and marketing communications, it achieves high awareness, favourability and

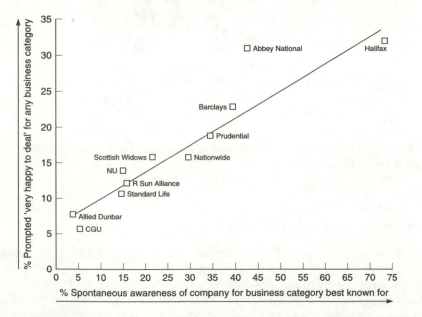

Figure 19.7 Overall propensity to deal with financial companies correlates with their spontaneous brand awareness for the category of business for which they are best known. (*Source*: Ipsos-RSL SyFT, 1999)

likeability. If its does these really well, then the next step for the brand is to create a reputation for living up to its promises. Doing this will establish real customer trust. Advertising and marketing communications are also essential to achieving this position.

The importance of trust

This public trust in the brand can be a very powerful asset should the corporation be called upon to defend itself, for example in the case of a product contamination or due to the actions of a rogue employee. As a result of its long-term investment in its brand equity, Ford will probably emerge relatively unscathed, when Firestone Tyres, the other party involved in the product liability cases in the USA, may not.

Using mass communications to make public promises, which the organisation then has to live up to, is a highly effective way to achieve a stretch target and establish trust. But woe betide the company which makes such a promise in public and fails through its behaviour to keep it!

In the same way, advertising and other forms of marketing communications are a powerful method of establishing customer charters and guarantees. Being clear about codes of conduct or corporate 'brand manners' manages the expectations of all the stakeholders who are involved with the corporation, and enables the brand to deliver outstanding customer satisfaction.

The John Lewis Partnership, Kwikfit, The Carphone Warehouse and Pret à Manger are all leading corporate brands who communicate customer charters as a key ingredient in their promise.

Communicating the company story to build morale

A consistent and engaging 'story' effectively told by the leaders of the corporation, retold by its employees and made public by advertising, helps enormously in motivating the whole organisation and aligning its efforts behind common goals. The corporate 'story' as communicated through advertising, websites, public relations or events creates drama, excitement and momentum. These are especially important elements in building and maintaining employee morale. Companies which give their people more than material reasons to 'get out of bed in the morning' reap enormous rewards in terms of increased employee commitment.

The Co-operative Bank's decision to make investments only in ethical companies, and to articulate this stance consistently in its advertising and its behaviour, has been supported very strongly by its employees. The results of their staff survey in Figure 19.8 demonstrate how fully they support their brand:

Figure 19.8 Results of The Co-operative Bank's staff survey

97% satisfied with banks' decision on ethical policies
97% believe stance has a direct effect on customer recruitment
89% believe it has a direct effect on customer retention
89% feel proud to be an employee of The Co-operative Bank
88% perceive the company to be a responsible member of society
87% feel business is mindful of its impact on the environment
82% believe stance has a positive effect on customer service

Source: The Co-operative Bank Employee Survey, March 1998

Tesco, with its focus on employees and attention to retail detail, has encapsulated its work ethic in the copyline, which originated in its advertising, but has now permeated the entire organisation and has become its ethos. There is no doubt that the consistent focus on 'Every Little Helps' has been instrumental in helping Tesco achieve brand leadership in one of the most competitive of all UK market sectors. At the same time this outstanding retailer's long-running 'Computers for Schools' cause-related marketing programme has added a valuable higher-order benefit to the prosaic activity of shopping, for employees and customers alike.

Conclusions

For a corporate brand to succeed in the modern social, economic and political environment, it has to concentrate on doing three interrelated things really well: being famous, being likeable and being consistent (Figure 19.9). Effective advertising and marketing communications, linked to consistent and transparent corporate behaviour, are fundamental to achieving all three.

Figure 19.9 The three interrelated requirements for success

The argument in brief: Chapter 20

- This chapter argues that a 'new breed' of brands are emerging that are far removed from the conventional, often fmcg, brands that dominate traditional thinking.
- For these 'non-conventional' brands a new set of rules is needed, both for how we view and evaluate such brands, but also how we characterise the buying decision process for them.
- The chapter suggests that, for these brands, 'subscription' is a more valuable descriptor than 'buying', and the 'subscription decision process' is described.
- Finally, the chapter examines what the role for advertising might be at each stage of that process, and how overall, therefore, it can add value to non-conventional brands too.

Chapter 20

Advertising and the non-conventional brand

Leslie Butterfield

Introduction

All the other chapters in this book (and most of the examples within each) concern advertising for commercial product or service brands. Indeed the majority of these examples are of what we might call 'traditional' brands: they exist (particularly in the fmcg world) as simple, physical products that you buy, use and (hopefully) buy again. Of course there are examples, too, of more 'complex' brands – cars, airlines, retailers, credit cards – and the role of advertising in categories such as these is clearly more complex too.

What hasn't really featured elsewhere – and yet is a subject of growing interest – is what role advertising can play for what we might call 'non-conventional' brands.

What do we mean by 'non-conventional brands'?

Figure 20.1 shows a typology of different kinds of brand. It is not intended to be comprehensive but rather illustrative of the scope and diversity of brands in today's world. The brand types (with examples in each case) sit along a spectrum that runs from simple to complex, from easily identified to more ethereal, and from tangible to intangible. My contention is that as one moves down this

Simple/ identified/ tangible	Type	Example
	1 Brands that exist as simple physical products	Birds Eye Frozen Peas
	2 Ditto, but come with an 'attitude'	Virgin, Nike
	3 Products that come with a 'package' of other services/relationship brands	Cars, AMEX
	4 Retailer brands	Tesco
	5 Ingredient brands	Intel
	6 Services with tangible manifestations/benefits	AA, NHS, holidays
	7 Services with intangible manifestations/benefits e.g. security/peace of mind	Insurance, banking, trade unions
	8 Services that one engages with or uses tacitly	Charities, Inland Revenue, Metropolitan Police
	9 'People' brands	Politicians, personalities, CEOs
	10 'Higher order entity' brands	Countries, regions, the Church of England, the justice system
Complex/ ethereal/ intangible	11 'Idea' brands	Royalty, Islam

Figure 20.1 A typology of brands

spectrum, particularly beyond the mid-way point, one encounters more and more brands that do not fall easily within the conventional definitions of a brand.

That, indeed, as a result of the nature of the relationship they seek with their users, or the timescale of that relationship or even the way in which they would define 'users', these brands behave very differently from traditional brands. Hence the label 'non-conventional'.

Defining the non-conventional brand (NCB)

The implication here is that to embrace these new types of brand we need a new type of brand definition, one that recognises that brands generally can and should be more broadly defined than some of the 'classic' definitions in the marketing literature. Here's how such a definition might look:

A brand can be anything from which the people who interact with it can or may in the future derive some kind of 'value' or express some element of their identity, and from which the delivering organisation seeks to gain value, sometimes monetary, sometimes not.

A number of points here:

- There is an implied transaction here between user and provider, but it may be entirely an emotional one.
- Identity, and hence identification, may be a substantial part of that transaction.
- The transaction may not involve a purchase.
- While the 'interaction' may occur today, its 'value' may arise some way into the future.
- The audience to whom the brand is addressing itself may never be 'users' in the traditional sense.

So what kinds of brands are we talking about here, that sit within this 'extended' definition?

Well, at the very least, they may be the *most* complex types of 'traditional' brand:

- Retailers
- Tangible services
- Ingredient brands.

But in fact, the area that we're most interested in here are organisations, institutions or individuals in the bottom half of our typology that (a) may have only recently woken up to the reality of their 'branded status' or (b) may indeed never have thought about themselves as brands at all.

In the first category might come brands that are struggling to define or redefine their purpose. Examples here might include:

- The Co-operative Movement
- The TUC
- The NHS
- The Conservative Party
- The Police
- The Salvation Army
- The Church of England, etc.

In the second category come those who might be surprised (or even offended) by the word 'brand' being applied to them:

- Politicians
- (some) Charities

- An organisation's CEO
- A specific TV programme
- The Criminal Justice System
- Apprenticeships
- Individual trade unions
- Countries, regions, towns, streets
- Religions (e.g. Islam), etc.

Many of these brands are ones where the benefits they deliver may be to society as a whole, and hence beyond the specific individuals they interact with. In other words, they may have a direct relationship with employees, members, users, or stakeholders but they seek or require support from a wider sector of society.

Why are NCBs different from 'traditional' brands?

As the above examples demonstrate, these are not necessarily brands I buy (or even consume). They may be somewhere I visit or live, a (free) service I use, something I may or may not believe in, something that comes out of my taxes, an organisation I may need in the future, etc. My interaction may be different too – not a purchase, rather an encounter, a temporary 'overlap' with my life, a resource I might need to be aware of etc. So the 'term' (i.e. timescale) of the relationship with that brand may be different – long-term, back-of-mind presence, infrequent or remote use (e.g. as a donor or supporter). Hence too, my expectations may be different. Less about utility, more about reliance, trust, even permanence.

As a result, just as 'classic' brand definitions are insufficient, so too are 'classic' buying decision process models. And hence the role for advertising for brands such as these may be radically different too.

Advertising and the classic buying decision process

For most routine brand buying decisions, the process that is often postulated is a very simple one (see Figure 20.2). Simple, perhaps, to the point of simplistic – particularly since this kind of process parallels the equally simple 'advertising effect' models developed in the USA in the 1960s. Here's a typical example:

| Awareness ⟶ Interest ⟶ Desire ⟶ Action |

Although still widely used, most advertising practitioners would view this 'stepwise' model as being somewhat naïve:

(a) Because consumers' relationships even with product brands are much more complex than this.
(b) Because brands exist partly to habituate behaviour.
(c) Because communications work in more, and more subtle, ways than this step-wise model would suggest.

And if this model is simplistic for product brands, it's probably of no use at all for our non-conventional brands. Why? Because the brands we're talking about here may not be 'needed', bought, exist in repertoires, satisfy desires or be used twice.

They may even be what I call 'long-distance brands', seeking to develop a relationship with you now even if you're unlikely to use them for perhaps decades into the future. (Think of brands like the Samaritans, Funeral Providers, Nursing Homes, Saga, etc.)

They may be trying to reach others (users perhaps) *through* you, because you may be influential on or a peer to the person they actually want to reach. (Think of the Catholic Church, the Scouts, universities even.)

It's precisely because of these extended timescales and extended audiences that we need the kind of extended brand definition that we touched on earlier.

Finally, and perhaps *most* importantly is the fact that these brands don't wait on shelves for you to approach them, they often approach you, like strangers offering a hand. And, in approaching you, they may be seeking not purchase, but *subscription*.

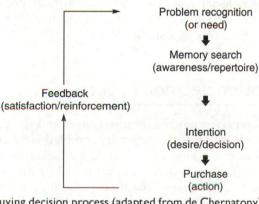

Figure 20.2 The buying decision process (adapted from de Chernatony)

The concept of 'subscription'

Almost all our historic thinking about brands involves some kind of monetary exchange. But, as our earlier 'extended' definition pointed out, non-conventional brands may not. Put simply, rather than asking you to buy them, they may just be asking you to 'buy into' them, or what they stand for. Hence the notion of 'subscription', because what in fact these brands may be asking you to do is:

- Donate to them (time, money or goods)
- Approve of them
- Remember them
- Support them
- Feel positive towards them
- Oppose something they oppose
- Use them in the future
- Own them remotely
- Live in or visit them or otherwise
- Allow them into your life, now or in the future.

What's more, as already intimated above, these brands may approach you more as people than as products. In other words, there is learning to be had from the world of interpersonal relationships, and how these are formed, in understanding how brands like these should communicate to gain 'subscription'. First impressions, non-verbal communications, tone-of-voice, attractiveness, empathy, body language – all of these may inform our thinking about the optimum 'behaviour' of our non-conventional or 'subscription' brands.

The implication of this is that, at the very least, we may need a new, still simple, (but not simplistic) model of the 'subscription decision process' for these kinds of brands. And this in turn will help us to define what role advertising can play in generating that subscription.

The 'subscription decision process'

Work that I have done on countries, issues, causes and charities, political parties and people brands confirms the generally accepted view that two of the key drivers of identification – a kind of surrogate for 'subscription' – are 'awareness' (have I heard of them?) and 'familiarity' (do I know anything about them?). But drawing from some of the theory about how inter-personal relationships are formed, I would interpose between these two in our subscription process 'visualisation' (do they conjure up an immediate picture?).

Moving beyond these three, I would now postulate the following steps in the process of subscription:

- Resonance: do they 'mean' anything to me? Are they relevant to my life?
- Disposition: frankly, do I like them, or at least empathise with them?

Figure 20.3 The subscription decision proces

Leading to:

■ Subscription: will I use, visit, support, etc. this brand at a relevant moment?

Figure 20.3 shows how the subscription process looks in total.

What role can advertising play in this process?

The subscription process described here is not a simple 'stepwise' model (like our earlier AIDA example). That's because each of the 'stages' in the process is both cumulative and 'deepening'. As such, advertising's role will vary at each stage – and (very generally) will be more effective at the 'upper' stages; whereas at the 'deeper' stages other factors (word of mouth, one's own value system, etc.) may be the dominant influences. That said, let's look briefly at how advertising might work at each stage:

■ **Awareness**:
The most obvious role for advertising: creating simple name awareness and linking it to the relevant subject.
■ **Visualisation**:
More difficult, but powerful if achieved. Advertising can give people a positive picture, or iconic image that they can immediately 'conjure' when the name is recalled. (Comic Relief would be a good example here.)
■ **Familiarity**:
Maybe just one fact, value or impression that 'connects' quickly with that brand. Prompting the response: 'I know them; don't they do X?' Through clarity of pro-

position, and powerful expression of the brand's essence, advertising can perhaps create the 'memorable parcel' of images that will endure to a distant point of need.

■ **Resonance**:
More complex, because in a sense this is down to the user to make the connections. Advertising's role here might be to stress those actions, behaviours or values that are likely to have the greatest or widest 'draw'. Given, though, that the future is less certain than the past, advertising's role here may be to stress tomorrow's needs rather than yesterday's experience.

■ **Disposition**:
Hard for advertising to influence in terms of content (what it says). Importantly though, through execution (how it says it), advertising can disarm, give humanity, raise a smile – all of which can affect the 'attractiveness' of our brand, and hence 'liking'.

■ **Subscription**:
The end-point of all the above. Because the process is cumulative, advertising is working towards this point rather than addressing it directly. That said, advertising may have a role here in providing a call to action in terms of support/donation/membership, etc., or to maintain/refresh emotional subscription over the long term.

Conclusion

It's early days for these kinds of brands, and for this kind of model. Indeed the literature in this area seems pretty impoverished. So the concept of 'subscription', and the process it implies, might help in the appreciation that, for many organisations, traditional 'buying' models are inappropriate. In this new world of brands, a new approach is needed – one that is sensitive to the subtleties of organisations that are often at the beginning of their journey into the communications arena. The subscription decision process model outlined here perhaps represents a valuable first step along that road. And the role of advertising postulated at each stage will perhaps help the 'brand owners' in these organisations to identify and develop new and more imaginative ways to deploy this most powerful of communications vehicles.

Index

Marketing titles from Butterworth-Heinemann

Student List

Creating Powerful Brands (second edition), Leslie de Chernatony and Malcolm McDonald
Direct Marketing in Practice, Brian Thomas and Matthew Housden
eMarketing eXcellence, PR Smith and Dave Chaffey
Fashion Marketing, Margaret Bruce and Tony Hines
Innovation in Marketing, Peter Doyle and Susan Bridgewater
Integrated Marketing Communications, Tony Yeshin
Internal Marketing, Pervaiz Ahmed and Mohammed Rafiq
International Marketing (third edition), Stanley J. Paliwoda and Michael J. Thomas
Key Customers, Malcolm McDonald, Beth Rogers and Diana Woodburn
Marketing Briefs, Sally Dibb and Lyndon Simkin
Marketing in Travel and Tourism (third edition), Victor T. C. Middleton with Jackie R. Clarke
Marketing Plans (fifth edition), Malcolm McDonald
Marketing: The One Semester Introduction, Geoff Lancaster and Paul Reynolds
Market-Led Strategic Change (third edition), Nigel Piercy
Relationship Marketing (second edition), Martin Christopher, Adrian Payne and
    David Ballantyne
Relationship Marketing for Competitive Advantage, Adrian Payne, Martin Christopher,
    Moira Clark and Helen Peck
Relationship Marketing: Strategy & Implementation, Helen Peck, Adrian Payne,
    Martin Christopher and Moira Clark
Strategic Marketing Management (second edition), Richard M. S. Wilson and Colin Gilligan
Strategic Marketing: Planning and Control (second edition), Graeme Drummond and
    John Ensor
Successful Marketing Communications, Cathy Ace
Tales from the Market Place, Nigel Piercy
The CIM Handbook of Export Marketing, Chris Noonan
The Fundamentals of Advertising (second edition), John Wilmshurst and Adrian Mackay
The Fundamentals and Practice of Marketing (fourth edition), John Wilmshurst and
    Adrian Mackay
The Marketing Book (fifth edition), Michael J. Baker (ed.)
The New Marketing, Malcolm McDonald and Hugh Wilson
Total Relationship Marketing (second edition), Evert Gummesson

Forthcoming

Marketing Logistics (second edition), Martin Christopher and Helen Peck
Marketing Research for Managers (third edition), Sunny Crouch and Matthew Housden

Marketing Strategy (third edition), Paul Fifield
Political Marketing, Phil Harris and Dominic Wring

Professional List

Cause Related Marketing, Sue Adkins
Creating Value, Shiv S. Mathur and Alfred Kenyon
Cybermarketing (second edition), Pauline Bickerton and Matthew Bickerton
Cyberstrategy, Pauline Bickerton, Matthew Bickerton and Kate Simpson-Holley
Direct Marketing in Practice, Brian Thomas and Matthew Housden
e-Business, J. A. Matthewson
Effective Promotional Practice for eBusiness, Cathy Ace
Essential Law for Marketers, Ardi Kolah
Excellence in Advertising (second edition), Leslie Butterfield
Fashion Marketing, Margaret Bruce and Tony Hines
Financial Services and the Multimedia Revolution, Paul Lucas, Rachel Kinniburgh and
    Donna Terp
From Brand Vision to Brand Evaluation, Leslie de Chernatony
Go to Market Strategy, Lawrence Friedman
Internal Marketing, Pervaiz Ahmed and Mohammed Rafiq
Marketing Made Simple, Geoff Lancaster and Paul Reynolds
Marketing Professional Services, Michael Roe
Marketing Strategy (second edition), Paul Fifield
Market-Led Strategic Change (third edition), Nigel Piercy
The Channel Advantage, Lawrence Friedman, Tim Furey
The CIM Handbook of Export Marketing, Chris Noonan
The Committed Enterprise, Hugh Davidson
The Fundamentals of Corporate Communications, Richard Dolphin
The Marketing Plan in Colour, Malcolm McDonald and Peter Morris
The New Marketing, Malcolm McDonald and Hugh Wilson

Forthcoming

Marketing Logistics (second edition), Martin Christopher and Helen Peck
Marketing Research for Managers (third edition), Sunny Crouch and Matthew Housden
Marketing Strategy (third edition), Paul Fifield
Political Marketing, Phil Harris and Dominic Wring

For information on all these titles, as well as the ability to buy online, please visit
www.bh.com/marketing